One Day, I Will Be Successful

I have tried it, and it works!
Now it's your turn to try.

One Day, I Will Be Successful

Practical Ways to Create Fun in Your Life as well as Abundance, Prosperity, and Happiness

Haresh Buxani

PARTRIDGE
A Penguin Random House Company

To order additional copies of this book, contact
Toll Free 800 101 2657 (Singapore)
Toll Free 1 800 81 7340 (Malaysia)
orders.singapore@partridgepublishing.com

www.partridgepublishing.com/singapore

In very rare moments in our lives, perhaps by chance or more than chance, we meet someone with a truly unique life. Haresh Buxani is one such special person. He was my patient, but now he is also my good friend.

The coincidence of our meeting—an appointment ordained by God Almighty, a God-incident for certain—has made me marvel at life in a more spiritual way, because, for Haresh, life is a vivid reality.

When we first met, Haresh had all the odds stacked against him. His medical problems were increasing by the minute and often seemingly insurmountable. But today, several years later, Haresh lives to tell his story—one that is full of real-life motivational secrets. Importantly, he does this in a very warm and personal manner, which is precisely his character.

If you are in a life-changing encounter where you seem to be pushed into the corner, this book is for you. Though the prose is simple, the message is deep and real. Do not mistake its brevity for a lack of content. There are loads of hidden treasures neatly and perfectly packaged for those who, perhaps because of similar difficult circumstances, are ready to take in information only in smaller portions.

To Haresh, my friend, *good job*!

To those who read this book, may Haresh motivate you to believe that you will succeed, one day at a time.

Dr. Gerrard K. H. Teoh
MBBS, MMed (Internal Medicine), FAMS (Hematology)
Hematologist (fellowship in immunohematology, Harvard)

This little book packs a lot of successful advice. In fifty essays, you will learn simple strategies that can lighten your spirits, expand your mind, enhance your life, and broaden your perspective. This book can help improve you and your good self.

Contents

Foreword

There are lessons in life that simply can't be taught. There are situations in life that are simply not in our hands, yet life goes on. To those who feel overwhelmed by circumstances or simply feel that there is no light in sight, I say, "Read this book." It will give you hope and some invaluable tips to help you move on.

I salute Haresh J. Buxani for having the courage and wisdom to write about his circumstances and what he had to deal with; under the same circumstances, many of us would have easily given up. Let this book be an inspiration to many.

God bless.

Haresh Vatwani, a good friend of the author

Preface

This is not a book on the secrets of investment. I am not a famous speaker, and neither am I a doctor, nutritionist, psychologist, mechanic, chef, or someone who feels qualified to tell you how to build an airplane. Actually, this book is about my experiences in life, and I share them with you in the hope that you will use them to achieve something in your life and be a successful person. Although this book is my first attempt at writing, I hope to show you, through my life experiences, how to do practical things to create fun in your life as well as how to create abundance, prosperity, and happiness.

I began writing this book in June 2008 after my good friend, Haresh Vatwani, who lives in Singapore, persuaded me to write my life story. I had been turning him down, as I had no interest in doing so. And I did not know how to start writing a book. One day, I was watching Season Three of *The Biggest Loser* on television. (I usually watched every episode, and I tried not to miss the exercise episode.) Every day, I heard the announcer ask viewers, "Tell me your story about the Biggest Loser."

That was what prompted me to start writing this book.

Acknowledgments

To my late father,
Jaikishin Buxani
This is what I should have said to you when I was younger.
"Dad, may your soul rest in peace. We all love and miss you so dearly."
"Dad, we miss you."
"Dad, we love you."
Dad,
You passed away at a very young age.
I have many stories to tell you,
Though I'm not sure where to begin.
I could write a billion pages,
Even though I do know
You won't be able to read them.
You can see from above
That we are fine and doing well.
Dad, you're a loving father
With a heart of gold.
Each day of my life,
I remember you day and night.
I remember all that you have taught us.
Thank you for taking good care of us when we were young,
So today I have written my life's experience.

Please bless my first book, *One Day, I Will Be Successful,* and the
countless people who read it.

* * *

To my mother,
Indra

Mum, without you, there would be no *One Day*.
Your love, attention, and guidance have made me who I am.
You showed me the way to serve and to accomplish many things.
Without you, there would be nothing I could
ever fulfill, no matter how hard I tried.
Because of you, I have love, joy, sadness, contentment,
smiles, laughter, satisfaction, and peace.

Thank you, Mum.

I have always loved you. You are a gift from God.

* * *

To my dear one,
Brother Kishore K. J. Buxani

Thank you for your moral support, care, and love, for which I thank God—brilliant younger brother who has given me a gift of priceless love, which has enabled me to look at life positively. Also to my sister-in-law, Pia K. J. Buxani, who is dear to me. I call her sister, and she calls me brother. We have a good, close friendship. She is an intelligent person who believes in a positive lifestyle. And I can't forget my two charming nephews, who create such fun within our family, which in turn creates happiness for all of us.

In addition, I have twenty very good friends: Laurence Wee, Vinit Chhabra, Sunil D. Chainani, Harry R. Chainani, Haresh Vatwani, Ashok Advani, Jit Nagpal, Arvind Chanana, Bob Singh, Ishvinder Singh Bajaj, Havinder Singh Bajaj, Vinod Kumar, Edward Seah, Vincent Tandiono, and the ladies Ms. Grace Tan, Ms. Gladys Wee, Ms. Strawberry, Ms. Coco, Ms. Jo Lee Soo Hoon, and Mrs. Irene Lim Suan Kim, president of the Lupus Association (Singapore), from 2011 onward. I have known some of these great friends for years, and our friendship is priceless. They look after themselves well and are always looking at life with a positive mind-set.

My wonderful family consists of many cousins who are loving and dear to me. I also thank my eight favorite doctors: Professor Leong Keng Hong, Dr. Gerrard K. H. Teoh, Dr. Grace Lee, Dr. Mak Koon Hau, Dr. Sriram Shankar, Dr. Tan Chai Beng, and their team members based at Gleneagles Hospital in Singapore. And there are two more: one from Singapore General Hospital, Dr. S. G. Tan, and Dr. Mohammad Tauqeer Ahmad from the Raffles Hospital. They are excellent and brilliant doctors, and meeting them was worth every penny.

Last but not least, I thank Mr. Trevor Binedell and Ms. Yvonne Hwong, YS, my two angels who work at the Tan Tock Seng Hospital's Foot

Care and Limb Design Center in Singapore. It is the only center with a specialized workshop that makes and assembles customized prosthetics.

The Foot Care and Limb Design Center's head of the prosthetics and orthotics department, Mr. Trevor Binedell, and physiotherapist Ms. Yvonne Hwong, YS, took very good care of my prosthetic right leg, and I call them angels of God, as they were the ones who guided me in how to walk again. All of them put in a lot of effort getting me, their patient, back to having a normal way of life again. God bless them always.

I want to say a big thank-you to all the people above for their positive thinking, generosity, and creative ideas.

I love you all!

Thank you, God, for joy and good health, sadness and sickness, and the happiness, prosperity, and contentment you have given me.

Introduction

I remember my words when I woke up that day in early June 2008. I had been admitted to the hospital. That very day, my right leg had to be amputated, and there was nothing I could do—nothing—as it was beyond my control.

The doctors in the hospital could not figure out why both of my legs were swollen below the knee. I did not have any of the symptoms of a disease that would cause me to lose my legs, such as hypertension (high blood pressure), diabetes, heart problems, kidney problems, or high cholesterol. At one point, I even lost my voice and had blurred vision for about two hours. That's when I was admitted to the hospital. The stroke ward doctors confirmed that I had suffered a mild stroke, and three weeks later, my lung was clotted, my brain was clotted, and my legs were still swollen. I remember that my right leg was chilled below the knee.

My family members and a family friend, Laurence Wee had been beside me since I was admitted, and I received much moral support, care, and love from them, for which I thank God.

The doctors at the hospital advised me that they needed to amputate my right leg below the knee. This was not an easy decision, and I had very little time to make it. I realized that I had no choice, as the surgeon already informed me that, I have only FIVE DAYS to live.

I was in shocked!

But to allow the doctors to amputate, as I could feel the limb becoming numb, and the skin was changing color by the day. I was diagnosed with the critical illnesses systemic lupus erythematosus (SLE) and antiphospholipid syndrome (APS). What are SLE and APS sickness in medical terms?

- Systemic lupus erythematosus (SLE), better known as lupus, is an autoimmune disease where the body's immune system becomes hyperactive and attacks normal, healthy tissue. This results in symptoms such as inflammation, swelling, and damage to joints, skin, kidneys, blood, and the heart and lungs. People with lupus are often referred to and managed by a specialist, usually a rheumatologist or doctors.

- Antiphospholipid syndrome (APS) is sometimes called Hughes syndrome. It affects the blood, making it more likely to clot. This can lead to blood clots (called thrombosis) forming in blood vessels, making APS a serious illness. People with APS are often referred to and managed by a specialist, usually a hematologist (a blood specialist) or rheumatologist (a specialist in bone, joint, and soft-tissue disorders and certain autoimmune diseases).

Ten days later, while I was still in the hospital, I began asking, "Why is this happening to me? Why do I have to go through all this?" I cried the entire day; I believe I was depressed. On the morning of the eleventh day, I told myself, "One fine day, I will walk again. I will do brisk walks, and I will run." I kept myself from crying and said that if I could walk properly again, that would be enough.

Without my family's support, there would be no such fine day. Their love, attention, and guidance strengthened my soul to lift myself out or the depression and allow me to look toward a better life. My family showed me love and care, and I thank God for the joy and good health, sadness and sickness, and for happiness. I thank God for giving me five great doctors in Singapore, who took good care of my illness.

Despite having a potentially serious illness, I refused to allow circumstances to affect my outlook on life negatively.

My family members always told me, "We must remember we are on earth only once. What good we can do, we do it now." We must remember to meditate and stay focused during our journey. This and the book *The Monk Who Sold His Ferrari*, by Robin Sharma, helped me to come out of the depression I was going through.

I began writing this book in June 2008. It is about my experiences, and I would love to share it with everyone, including both successful and unsuccessful people. I hope you will use it to achieve something in life and be a successful person. Although this book is my first attempt at writing, I can show you, through my experiences, how to create fun in practical ways as well as how to create abundance, prosperity, and happiness through your thoughts.

It took me six years to complete this book, and I am now looking for a local publisher in the hope of providing a source of aid, encouragement, and comfort to those suffering the same fate as I have.

***

In addition, I wrote an article called "I Have Been Diagnosed with Lupus. What Should I Do Next?" for the February 2013 issue of the Lupus Association (Singapore) publication.

In life, we have two options: we can be miserable and ask, "Why did this happen to me?" or we can stay positive and be thankful for the things we still have. I make an effort to stay optimistic and remain confident in the team of doctors and nurses that tend to me.

I started the Marina Bay Walking Meetup group on June 4, 2012. This walking group has more than 3,030 members from all walks of life. We walk every Saturday morning at various locations in Singapore. A month later, I founded the Walk for Lupus walking group. This group walks once every two months at around sunset, because all lupus patients are sensitive to the sun, and the majority have skin diseases. The walks are great opportunities for staying healthy and making new friends. I am also a volunteer with the Lupus Association (Singapore).

On World Lupus Day 2013, the Marina Bay Walking Meetup group walked 3.5 kilometers along the Marina Bay Waterfront Promenade. On May 10, 2014, the main organizer of the Lupus Association (Singapore) and the co-organizer of the Marina Bay Walking Meetup group organized our first charity Walk for Lupus at the Botany Center within Singapore Botanic Garden. We managed to get almost S$50,000 donation from the public, who took part in walking 1.9 kilometers on the Heritage Trail. All the proceeds were given to the Lupus Association (Singapore).

There is a need to create and increase public awareness about lupus, as few have heard about it or have knowledge about it, unlike common diseases such as cancer. It is also important for patients to explore ways to cope with the stress of suffering from lupus. Frequent exercise and relaxation make it easier for lupus patients to battle the disease. Exercise not only reduces stress and lifts a person's spirits, but it also improves sleep. Stay active and positive always. May you be blessed with good health!

Who Can Benefit from Reading This Book?

One Day is written for successful people, unsuccessful people, patients, and people from all walks of life, those who have given up on life, and those who are *not sure how to achieve success in the world in which we live.*

When was the last time you read a book?

Reading regularly is keeps us motivated. We need to be positive. We need to be motivated to learn to create abundance, prosperity, success, and much more for ourselves.

We also need to inform teenagers how powerful our minds really are. Some teenagers are already doing quite well creating goals and setting up their own investments and businesses to become successful entrepreneurs. They simply believe in themselves; they believe they can do what they dream. That is all anyone needs to do.

Here is one thing we must remember: we are here on earth only once. Whatever good we can do, we do it now. We must remember to meditate and stay focused in our journey. Believe me, that's what works! We must not forget our goals, as they give us balance and motivate us toward success. Balanced ensures that our health, heart, relationships, mental state, and life in general are in good order. Take your life, enjoy it, and create happiness around you. Then watch how you achieve success. Don't worry about how it is going to happen.

* * *

Do you know that we can find abundance easily anywhere and everywhere?

We just need to broaden our mind and think more acutely in order to be successful people. If you do not believe you can do it, I believe you can. It is possible. You could have an entrepreneurial spirit within you. Find it and learn to hear your own voice instead of other people's voices. When *you* practice visual thinking, the strategies will come to you.

Do not be afraid to fall in love with what you do. Just be a creator, and begin your visualization.

Yes, I believe in you.

You will benefit when you produce a solution and create strategies for yourself and others. You will learn to apply the key objective of a life in harmony.

The One Day Method of strategic thinking awaits you within this book. The following are just brief instructions and techniques.

To create your new goals, you have to take action. But first you need to understand the big picture.

Please turn the pages and read on.

Saw it, in one magazine.

One

The Most Important Secrets in Life

The instructions in *One Day, I Will Be Successful* are simple to understand, and the techniques are easy to apply. Each chapter gives you safe, empowering ideas that allow you to overcome your old beliefs, forget past habits, and learn new habits of success. You will learn a new belief that will create abundance and success in your chosen path.

Furthermore, you will learn that you are able to plant in your subconscious mind the new seeds that create a successful lifestyle. There are a lot of benefits when you achieve something worthwhile after exploring the real world. Some of the ideas in this book can be used to bring about extraordinary and beneficial changes to your mind-set. Your level of thinking will be improved after you focus on this One Day Method. Your confidence and self-esteem will rise to a higher level. You will lose weight, be free of tension, and be able to manage your family life with ease.

You have been given the power of the mind and the ability to use these techniques to transform your dreams into a better life.

You would not have purchased this book unless you really wanted to make a change for the better. You have made the right choice in taking this step.

One last thing you must remember: you need motivation and faith in yourself. If you want to create anything in this life, it is possible, and you can do it.

By the way, have you written down an affirmation list? An affirmation list is a must, and the first step of the ten steps you have to take. You will be glad that you did it.

In life, everyone goes though experiences. If you still have fear and anger, you have to decide to either live with it or let it go. The choice is yours. Experiences are a learning experiment for your future expectations, which can sometimes be painful or horrible. Whatever happens, *you* can either let the fear go and move forward or keep it with you. No one can help you with what happened to you in the past.

Do not worry about having an affirmation list right now. Take your time, and write it when you feel ready and comfortable. You might want to read this book twice to understand it fully, and then start your list after that.

Two

Let's Start Our Remarkable Journey

Prosperity and happiness are what almost everyone wishes for, but not many have such wishes fulfilled. In our journey through life, there are always obstacles that keep us from achieving them.

You have a choice. You take either positive steps or negative steps. The best way to discover positive feelings within yourself is to begin to understand your inner feelings. To begin, take one baby step first, followed by another. Don't look back, and don't look ahead. Stay right in this moment. Take each step one by one, and focus on them over a thirty-day period. Stay positive. You will surprise yourself at what you can achieve in a short time. After that, continue again for another thirty days. This time try to visualize what you desire. Create the picture in your mind, and try to feel the beating of your heart—always staying focused on the results. This is one simple, positive plan that I always use to achieve any goal I have.

Once you understand these principles, they will allow you to feel happiness, delight, and contentment, regardless of the stress you may feel at work or the tension in your life right now.

Try it.

The key to prosperity, harmony, and happiness is in your mind and in your hands. Yes! It is definitely in your hands right now. Stop reading for two minutes, and look at both of your palms carefully. What do you see?

There are many stories, ventures, and connections as well as multiple lines of prosperity, happiness, success, trouble, marriage, and joy.

Have you ever thought about which affirmations you wish to have in your life? Think about these for five minutes and write them down. What have you always wished for?

Now put this affirmation list on a mirror, table, wall, or anywhere where you will see it often. If you read it every night before you go to sleep, your subconscious mind will make it a reality.

If you're 100 percent happy with every aspect of your life and do not want to change or learn anything new, close this book. But keep it under your pillow until you feel you really need it. This book could create a new mind-set for you, but only if you finish reading it. Your mind will then create abundant success only for you.

Three

Let's Explore How Our Mind Works

I want you to understand who you really are and how you fit into the big picture. Always remember, you need to explore as if you are a creator and you are always growing. The longer you live, the more your mind expands as you learn new ideas.

You need to acknowledge the world in which you live. You need to realize, for example, when you are driving on a road. You would like to get home quickly, as the traffic is heavy. Your friend in the passenger seat tells you to turn into the left lane, as there is a U-turn sign up ahead. And your friend in the rear seat tells you to turn right, as the venue is just five kilometers away.

You are feeling uncomfortable and frustrated, because you are not sure which direction to go. You keep looking at your watch, as you are late for an appointment, and the traffic is moving very slowly due because it's rush hour. You wonder whether you should make a U-turn and go back home or proceed to your destination. You need to make that choice *now* and are not sure what to do. No matter where you stand, you must think carefully, as you can see the U-turn not far ahead. Or are you going to choose to proceed to your destination?

Take one baby step first; do not look back or make the U-turn. Stay in the middle for the moment. Just stay where you are and proceed to your destination for your appointment. Contact the friend you are meeting, and tell him or her you have been delayed by an hour due to a traffic jam. Your friend will appreciate your call.

Take each step one by one, and stay focused. Do not think about what others are saying.

No matter where you stand, your choices are not limited. The choice you have to make is whether you want to feel bad for missing your appointment or you want to feel better for arriving for the appointment and having your friends wait in the car.

I want you to feel good in whatever decision you make. *You have to make a decision now.* Take the right step, and the natural law of attraction in the universe will support you.

Wherever you stand, you always have two choices. Make the right one, and you will feel better, because you have taken a step in the right direction. Do you know that in the next thirty days, you will know that the choices you have made are the right choices? This is all you need to do to manifest your dream—and you will feel great. Naturally, you have taken the right steps. You will be surprised. …

You are now learning to create a new habit and looking forward to the next thirty days, to your remarkable journey into a positive life. You need to stop going backward; rather, remain focused on going forward. That is all you need to do. I want you to begin to feel great about yourself. Dream of your future, and you will begin asking yourself when your dream will come to fruition.

Does this sound impossible? It's not. You will definitely achieve your dream.

Now you know why you haven't achieved your dream yet. It is because you were going about it the wrong way. Focus on the One Day Method, and forget the ways you were trying to achieve your goals. Start out positively, and do not feel miserable or feel that you can't achieve them. Stay focused on this method if you want to create what you really want.

Four

Eliminate What You Used to Do

Stop watching negative movies and stop talking to negative friends who have always told you what you can't do. Know what you want, and nature will create it for you. Feel the energy. Write down a list of positive goals before you go to sleep tonight. Write down your wishes. Focus on this method, and forget the past.

You can't do it both ways, as there is only one positive way, and this is it. Do you realize that you are just thirty days away from making your dream come true?

You need to create new law of attraction and create the ten wishes that you have in your mind right now. Think about the things you have always desired, and write them down. Remember to dream big. Visualize a good situation, and do not deviate from it. Concentrate only on the positive aspect of it, and bear the One Day Method in mind, not your previous method. Read your list of dreams before you go to sleep every night. Then pray for success, as prayers release power and create energy, so that when you wake up in the morning, you will feel a difference. You will be alert and will walk tall like a successful person.

Be positive, and forgive those who have hurt you. As you practice forgiveness, you will feel better about your life. You will be full of confidence and feel less of the burden that you have been carrying in your heart. You will be cheerful and positive. You will feel different about yourself. Look at the feelings that make you feel great. Feel the greatness, and all the good things will come to you—every morning.

Tell yourself, "I feel great, and I am thinking only about my goals today". Create a new wish list every day, and update your affirmation list every week.

Focus on your list, day and night. Take small baby steps to achieve your goals.

No matter how big or small your goals are, stick with them.

Five

Don't Panic

If your most important relationship is going well, pat yourself on the back for a job well done. You need to remember the most important lesson in the University of Life—that is, you need to be caring, to give more support, to respect others, to understand others better, and to understand financial problems and avoid all conflicts or upsetting situations, as life is too short. Stay happy.

If your relationship is going downhill or it's not working out well, don't panic. Try to make it good. If it still is not going well, take a three-day leave from work and go for a short vacation to think about you and what your next step is going to be. When you are alone in a nice, quiet place, you will be able to think better, as you will be able to have a conversation with the Almighty Superior above us. You can also talk to close friends or family members.

This is easy to say and hard to put into practice in the real world, but if you do not try, you will never know what lasting happiness is. So, take the steps that make you feel good. You will feel much better every day.

Six

Respect Your Values

Appreciate life, and appreciate your family members, especially your parents. Respect them, for they have never stopped caring for you. Do something different for them every year, and create joy for them, as your parents have worked very hard and saved every cent for you and your education. Do not leave them alone or leave them in a retirement home. Never ignore your parents. When was the last time you spoke with your mom and dad or celebrated their birthdays with them or taken them out to dinner or invited them to your home? Take this opportunity today to call your parents.

When was the last time you told your parents, "I love you"? If you have not told them that yet, what are you waiting for? Call your parents today and say something nice to them.

When you have done that, keep doing it; maintain a good relationship with them, because then you are taking good care of them. They will feel proud of you. However, if you have not been able to do that or can't think of any words to say to your parents, let me share with you three simple words: "I love you." With these words, you can tell them of the love you have for them and feel the magic feeling you get from them.

Try it. You have nothing to lose.

Always give thanks to God for happiness, prosperity, and your many other blessings. Give thanks to God for what you have, and believe that you can achieve.

***

Whether you are eight, eighteen, or eighty, you have room to improve yourself.

You can become better tomorrow than you are today.

As the Spanish proverb says, "He who does not look ahead remains behind"

Seven

Your Body Is a Temple

Look after your body, because your body is your temple. When you take care of your body, your body will take care of you.

What is the relationship between your mind and your body? When you know what you want, you can then alter your body's vibrations, as your body contains a massive amount of energy. When you begin to understand how you really feel, you will understand this better. You will be in charge of your feelings every day. Choose your thoughts wisely, as thoughts will turn into words.

When you were born into this world, your mind was wide open, and everything you saw was programmed in your mind. For example, if you put an African baby in a Chinese family, in the days and years that pass, the baby hears and sees how the Chinese speak, sit, behave, and dress, as well as their attitudes, how they save money, and their lifestyle. Would you believe the baby has been programmed?

One day, I spoke with this African, who is now a young boy and still living with the Chinese family. The boy spoke in Chinese as he sat down on a stool with his chopsticks in one hand and a rice bowl in the other. Chinese is all he knows how to speak, as that is his mother tongue. His subconscious mind had been programmed through what he saw and heard. He did not know the African language. He knew only how to behave as a Chinese person and speak Chinese.

How did this occur? It occurred because the subconscious mind controls your perception and your mind, and it accepts what it hears and sees. The boy was programmed to behave in a certain manner. And you can program yourself too. You can change your life.

But first you need to change your mind-set. As you guide yourself to think in a positive way and by practicing every day, you plant a new positive route in your mind, creating better future for yourself. Try to forget the misery of your past. Forget the old way, and concentrate only on how to program yourself using this new method. Always say, "I receive money from everywhere," and practice this paragraph every day. Speak and feel good about yourself. Believe it, and you will be successful one day.

People will see you differently and probably comment that you look different, and they will ask if you have found a new job or a new soul mate. Your reply will be, "No, nothing like that." They will then ask why you look so happy and where you found all your energy. Your reply will be, "Well, I'm happy because my life is moving in the right direction."

Do you know why I look happy? It is because I have forgiven someone, and I am thinking happy thoughts. I am taking the correct baby steps, which are the new way, and not the old ones anymore.

I look happy because I have made a wise choice and feel good about myself. I feel the good energy within me as I continue to program good and positive thoughts into myself. I have stopped thinking negatively, and now I think only in this new and positive manner, which makes me happy.

All the good things in my/your life will come soon.

Eight

The Mind—A Powerful Tool

Years back, I read an interesting book that a friend lent to me. I practiced the method in it and gained knowledge about how to manifest my own destiny and how to create real magic in my daily life. That book has helped me to find contentment. Some days, my life breaks down as obstacles come from various directions. I have learned how to turn the obstacles around as well as how to be happy and how to enter into a new dimension of life to further my spiritual growth.

Basically, the book explained that life is not our enemy, but our thinking can be. It said that our mind is a very powerful tool that can work for us or against us at any given moment. We have a choice. We can learn to flow with life, with loving and patient acceptance of our situation, or we can struggle against it.

A friend of mine advises me on occasionally that we are spiritual beings having a human experience. We have the capacity to make this human experience the best it can be. We have within us the resources to live a happy and fulfilled life regardless of the challenges we face. Her goal is to help me understand the real experience of a positive life by being more contented than I was before.

Understanding the principles of thought and how they apply throughout every aspect of my life is a valuable gift and a human experience.

I always applied the principles above, and I do achieve success.
You can too.

You may fail from time to time, but you must never give up.

Try again and again. One day, you will achieve the success you seek.

Nine

Baby Steps

Here's a brief look at how I use the Baby Steps Method. I practice my thoughts every day by looking at the positive lists I wrote while I was in the hospital. That changed my inner vision by creating a picture in my mind, which was the picture of the results. Honestly, by using the One Day Method and focusing on the baby steps, I changed my mind-set so that I focused only on a healthy lifestyle for my coming years.

I knew that I first had to let my right leg's knee stump heal, but at least I had an inner vision of a positive future, which I had created within me. I also received a number of down-to-earth facts on positive thinking from three of my caring family members: my brother, Kishore, my sister-in-law, Pia, and my good friend, Vinit, who is like a brother to me.

I went into a severe depression after a doctor told me that my leg would heal within two months, but it took four months. However, I was able to remove my negative feelings and focus on the areas that I needed to change. I explored my resources by looking at the seventeen items on my list and came up with a diet plan that covered a trial period of thirty days. I was proud of myself when I succeeded in completing the plan.

Today, six years later, I have succeeded more in my life journey. I have not completed everything on my list, but I am now happy, and I have accepted that all God has given me is good in some way. I feel that I am now a successful person.

I wanted to be even more successful in order to only my bigger dream in the list below. I manifested my own destiny with the moral support of my family members and with God's blessings. As Dr. Carlson claimed, our mind is a very powerful tool that can work for or against us at any moment.

It hit me one day that I wanted to achieve something in life. And since the mind is so powerful, I took the positive steps and began developing a positive attitude. I visualized that some things were possible for me to accomplish. I believed I could do it. I imagined I would be walking on the road one day with my new prosthetic leg and holding a black walking stick. This visualization helped to strengthen my mind so I could see the real picture before me in order to succeed.

Within six months, I managed to walk again. I kept on practicing in order to strengthen my walk and was blessed with the help of God. In addition, I give thanks to Ms. Yvonne, because she taught me how to walk properly again. I always call her Angel of God. I also thank Mr. Trevor for his advice on my prosthetic leg. He took good care of me.

Take action now, and you can have anything you want in life. Believe that you can do it. If you have not been successful before, you can be successful today after reading my book and taking baby steps to get there. However, to succeed, you need to first write down your wishes on a piece of paper with conviction.

Ten

My Special Message

At first, I didn't believe that my mind and brain could manifest
anything.

My attempt at imagining success failed many times.

I tried by visualizing and practicing that repeatedly.

I tried several times to visualize the list in my mind and focused on a
picture of success. After three years, I actually manifested my destiny.

You can too!

Eleven

Ask Yourself ...

Are you happy? Have you achieved the happiness that you longed for? Are you happy with the things you possess? Do you wish to be loved by someone? Are you successful? Are you enjoying abundance and prosperity? I hope that with this book you will achieve what you are thinking about right now. You can change your destiny, or you can just live with what you have now. The choice is yours.

As the author of this book, I can only pray and hope that one day you will be successful too.

What do abundance and prosperity mean to you? Money, a luxury vacation, a promotion, a vehicle, a house, a yacht, or something else that you dream of? If you want to attract abundance, success, prosperity, financial wealth, and much more, what do you need to do first? Work even harder than before or inherit a property from your grandparents?

Practical Ways to Create Fun in Your Life as Well as Abundance, Prosperity, and Happiness

First, you need to relax, stay calm, and meditate for thirty minutes each day. If you are not sure how to mediate, you can find free online meditation guidance.

Spend quality time with your family members. Go for a vacation or take them out during a weekend, and create fun, laughter, peace, and harmony. You will find that your mind is fully relaxed and clear of all negative thoughts.

Also clear the clutter from your home and workplace. And remove negativity from your life; throw it out with all the unwanted items. Think only of the law of attraction, recalling them at all times. Read your affirmation list daily, or at least once a week. In this way you will attract good things.

One thing I love about the law of natural attraction is that they actually guide you to manifest whatever you desire and create a positive energy toward our future prosperity and happiness. As soon as you wish for something and make a firm decision, these thoughts will send a signal to the universe. It may not happen tomorrow, and it may not happen in two weeks, and it will come to you when you least expect it. When you expect it to happen, it will not happen, and when you do not expect it to happen, it will take you by surprise. You will know when it has come.

Whatever we wish for, our powerful subconscious mind will make it happen. The universal spirit is with us every day. Once you know how to manifest it, you will not go back to your normal way of life. You can focus on the law of natural attraction to manifest a vehicle, a job, a property, an investment, a relationship, etc. Create something for yourself, and choose a positive path so that you do not fall back into negativity. Stop saying negative things (the old ways), and focus on talking positively (the new way). As you speak, your mind is in tune with you, appreciating what you have right now and focusing on the additional things.

Dreams come true.

Achieving goals is predictable; you just need to follow the recipe of success.

This book is your first baby step.

Twelve

Don't Deal with Problems; Find Solutions

Most people assume that the only way to solve a problem is to work on it. Deep down we all know that for every problem there is a solution.

Once you know how to manifest it, you will not go back to your normal way of life.

Focus on the law of natural attraction to manifest owning a vehicle, getting a job, making an investment, acquiring real estate, or improving your relationships. Create something for yourself, and choose a positive path so that you do not go back into negativity. Stop saying, "I have problems" (the old ways) and focus on talking positively (the new way). As you speak, your mind is in tune with you, appreciating what you have right now and beginning to focus on positive things.

What is the meaning of "law of attraction" and when was it discovered? According to Wikipedia,

> The *law of attraction* is the name given to the belief that "like attract like" and that by focusing on positive or negative thoughts, one can bring about positive or negative results. This belief is based upon the idea that people and their thoughts are both made from "pure energy", and the belief that like energy attracts like energy. One example used by a proponent of the law of attraction is that if a person opened an envelope expecting to see a bill, then the law of attraction would "confirm" those thoughts and contain a bill when opened. A

person who decided to instead expect a cheque might, under the same law, find a cheque instead of a bill.

The History: Thomas Troward, who was a strong influence in the New Thought Movement, claimed that precedes physical form and "the action of Mind plants that nucleus which, if allowed to grow undisturbed, will eventually attract to itself all the conditions necessary for its manifestation in outward visible form."

From 1901 to 1912 the English New Thought writer James Allen wrote a series of books and articles. He is best known for writing *As a Man Thinketh* in 1902. It's a good book to find and read.

The law of attraction has also been popularized in recent years by books and films such as *The Secret*. If you have not read or seen the movie, do so.

Thirteen

How Can I Be a Success?

Y ou know my One Day Method, but you may have to work hard to believe it. I have just finished my wishful thinking. You have read about the One Day method and about baby steps for looking at a positive life ahead. Now, let's see what you have learned so far:

- Your need a wish list. (Have you created one yet?)
- How is your positive life going? (Now it is your turn to visualize your future.)
- You must have dreams, too, so create your own.
- You can create opportunity and abundance for yourself and your family.

The next step is healthy eating and how you can be a success one day, experiencing abundance, prosperity, and happiness. There are three more secrets to what you need to do to be successful in life.

My secrets might change your life as well as your belief in your ability to become a better person, a person who respects his or her elders, a success.

You need to know how to balance these secrets for one day; when you do, you will be successful.

Fourteen

What Is Success?

Y ou will become what you think of yourself. First, you have to feel it and believe in it. Motivate yourself, and imagine a successful life. You can manifest something good just for yourself; you just need to visualize it sincerely and honestly.

If you think only about negative things, engage in negative talks, have negative energies, do not believe in anything, and have a fear of taking first steps, you might feel lousy, recall bad memories, and meet the wrong people. Talking negatively about past topics or engaging in gossip can degrade your inner feelings and just waste your time. You may also receive negative vibrations because of a negative mind as well as have the fear of baby steps and of achieving anything worthwhile. Fear, fear, fear …

One thing you must remember is that we come to earth only once in our lifetime, so now is the time to allow your dreams to come true. If not now, when will you take your first step? Take your fear and turn it into your friend. Get to know Mr. Fear better, and do not be afraid to invite him to be your best friend. If you can achieve this, I'm sure you will not have any problems with your next step of becoming a positive person and enjoying success in everything you do. Believe me and believe in yourself that fear is only your shadow.

Remember that.

Believe that you can do it no matter what. You will feel positive energies and positive feelings coming from within you, and you will feel positive thoughts coming from your inner strength.

Fifteen

Surround Yourself with Positive Friends

Feel the magical spirit coming from the universe right to you.

Develop new and positive friendships that will support you with courage by giving you a happy push into a positive life. You may feel different and unique, and you may feel extraordinary doing what you love. You may feel that the moment is now. You may have a passion for action and an emotional energy to face your new reality. You may feel the drive of a new optimism, and you look forward to each day with a new resolution.

What you need to do now is set the same goal for everything worthwhile you want to achieve. The key to a healthy life is to visualize joy, prosperity, happiness, and success in your mind right now. You need to create the desire … you need to be hungry for success … you need to focus fully and concentrate … you need to dream more and to turn the dream into reality … you need to take a deep breath and then exhale all the negatively from your life and inhale the positivity of the achievement have been dreaming of and which you are setting out to achieve. Create great energy filled with prosperity and abundance for you and your loved ones.

Let me explain how it works.

Do you know that the universe bends to your goals?

You must be happy. You must have goals. Without happiness, there are no goals. Remind yourself that we need goals in life, and you need your mind to shift. What is a mind shift?

First, you need to be happy, and your universal happiness can't be tied down to goals. You must be happy before you attain them, then the flow comes into the picture. Basically, you need to go into the flow; you need to be happy in the *now*. Happiness comes from the journey to your success. You need to discipline the happiness by reminding yourself every day. Many people go to work daily and earn less pay, and because of that, they are not happy. They can't get into that positive flow, because they are not happy!

You can manifest great vision, but your flow's impact won't happen simply because *you're not happy* in your job. So, if you don't enjoy what you're doing, you need to take a week off to think about your next step and about whether you would like to get out of that job. You need to be in a job that you are passionate about, so find that job you love. Then and only then will you succeed!

So, now we know that we have to stay happy to succeed before the real goals even come in our mind. We have four states of mind. Which state are you in now?

1. *Negative.* You may have a good career, but you are feeling depressed because of your salary or maybe because you are wearing a mask to impress others. If you spend too much of your time concentrating on your friends' lives, you eventually forget who you really are. My suggestion: Do not fear other people's judgments. Concentrate on who you are, and show the world the truth of who you are. Avoid being disappointed. If you can't get a girlfriend or boyfriend, don't worry. One fine day, I am sure you will get one. Maybe now is not the right time.

2. *Depressive.* Everything you touch, feel, or sense. You think you don't have any luck. Honestly, everyone has his or her own good luck. Come out from there and tell yourself, "I'm positive, and I can achieve my target"—and you will. You just need to say "I can" repeatedly so you can come out of the cocoon of negativity.

3. *Present.* Be happy in this moment. You have a great career, you own property, your married life is going well, but you are feeling boring.

4. *Successful.* You were born with a silver spoon in your mouth, but you feel lonely.

If you are in one of these states, don't worry so much. Concentrate on reading this book all the way through, and the answers will be in your mind in the next day or so. Then you will have started your new journey of having a successful life.

Feel the power.

Feel it, and engage the positive feelings with your good friends.

Believe in yourself.

Believe that you can do it.

It's possible.

Yes ... it's possible.

***

Pray

When we pray to God, we must be seeking nothing.
Don't pray when it rains if you don't pray when the sun shines.

Prayer is when you talk to God, and meditation is when you listen to God.

Pray not only because you need something
but because you have a lot to thank God for.

Amen.

***

What Is Next?

You need to be transformed and to begin to practice what you have learned so far. Enjoy this moment of greatness, of "One day, I will be successful."

You need to be hungry for prosperity and for success.

Only then will it work for you.

Sixteen

Healthy Eating Is a Must

Now let me share with you another side of the story, which is an important aspect of our daily life. Healthy eating is one of the best things you can do for yourself, because when we are healthy, we live longer, and we do not need to visit the doctor often.

All you need is a Microsoft Excel spreadsheet to draw up your own food chart and monitor your food and liquid intake daily (that is, how much you eat and how much liquid you drink each day). Follow only 98 percent of your diet plan; allow yourself a little indulgence. Eat a little unhealthy food now and then, which is called a cheat meal or a reward for yourself. Record your weight once a week.

Practice this method of calorie counting for one or two weeks only. Thereafter, your mind will take over, and you will understand what is good to eat and drink. Also, you do not have to have a spreadsheet to lose weight. Every technique in this book can be applied just as effectively with a pencil and paper.

I don't usually practice using the metric system or tedious preliminary studies, and I apologize to readers who do. I have learned to create a healthy meal and exercise plan in the simplest forms possible: food energy is calculated in kilojoules, the metric unit of energy. To convert kilojoules to kilogram calories ("food calories"), just divide by the kilojoules by 4.184. Simple knowledge works wonders.

I figured that in order to lose weight more quickly, I needed to eat even less. After a few weeks, however, I noticed that I was not losing weight as quickly as I thought I would. I became frustrated and upset with myself. Because I was really determined to continue losing weight, I had figured that I had to starve myself even more.

But my nutrition adviser, Ms. Helen said, "Let's *stop right there*! Let me explain what is going on inside the body and why eating less is not the answer." She said that the first step to losing weight was to rearrange my goals. Instead of thinking about losing weight, I must think about losing body fat and increasing or maintaining muscles, depending on my goals.

To help me lose weight, Ms. Helen once told me that when people want to lose weight, they often fast or skip meals. These people then feel pain and hunger. At first, they notice that they easily lose three to four kilos within the first week.

She told me to arrange my diet program to contain five to six meals a day of 38 to 42 percent carbohydrates, 42 to 50 percent proteins, 15 percent fats, and the rest fiber. She added that I should eliminate all junk food and processed food as well as sugar from my diet and opt for unprocessed, natural foods instead. Never ever starve or skip a meal. Missing out a meal is bad, and you would do well to remember that.

Basically it's a Weight Loss Method, for you to understand, your healthy eating which you going to start next week.

Before you start your healthy eating program. First you need to see where you are right now. Weigh yourself and note down in your Microsoft Excel spreadsheet as that will be your food and liquid monitor chart. You will need to record it down of what you eat each day and how much exercise you get. Once you start writing it down in your Microsoft Excel spreadsheet, you may learn things you never knew about your eating habits. You might be eating and drinking a lot of alcohol and have no idea at all. How much calories were in it. Understanding of what we eat daily gives you a sense of what needs to change.

The next step or shall I say, the next week weight loss method is really important for you. You have to make a long term healthy eating plan. If you're going to change your eating habits. You have to decide that you're motivated to make changes that will last for the rest of your life.

Read my book often. If your motivation is low. My book will give you extra motivation, that could jump-start your healthy eating programmed :)

Seventeen

A Simple Method for Staying Healthy

Cut down on bad fats and simple sugar calories, increase your water intake to a minimum of 2 liters and a maximum of 2.5 liters a day. Incorporate a sensible weight-training routine of three to four times per week. Do thirty minutes of exercise and thirty minutes of spiritual prayers. Have patience and allow some time for your body to burn off the unwanted body fat. Typically, you will be able to reduce your body's fat by 1.5 pounds a week at best, depending on your starting bodyweight, without sacrificing any muscle.

Please remember, when you are aiming to lose weight, do not make the most common mistake dieters make: eating less. Instead, consider losing fat and building muscle through proper dieting and exercise. This path will lead you to the lean and toned body of your dreams.

- Dieting without weight training = loss of fat and muscle = a smaller version of yourself; feeling flabby and weak

- Dieting with weight training = loss of fat and maintain muscle mass = a toned body

It's clear which the winner is.

Now let's recap.

- Dieting breaks down muscles.
- Weight training builds them.

- Weight training energizes you.
- Weight training makes you stronger.
- Weight training makes you less prone to lower back injuries.
- Strength gives you confidence and makes daily activities easier.
- Strength training is more beneficial than cardio workouts.

***

Plan to lose weight; start a week later.

Every other book encourages you to start your diet meal plan *now*.

But if you start immediately and drop it in a month, you have no real determination

Then why start?

Remember,

skipping meals, especially breakfast,
can actually make it more difficult to lose weight.

Do you know why?

Breakfast skippers tend to eat more food than usual at their next meal.

Eighteen

Going on a Diet

Wait one week before following your diet plan. During the week before you start, write your plan and goals in your smartphone or on a piece of paper that you tape on a wall, mirror, or cupboard. Look at the list every day and night. Think about it and visualize it, and it will become a reality in your subconscious mind. Think about your weight loss goal. Think about the healthy meals you are going to enjoy eating when you start to lose weight.

Plan your menu for each day of the next week, starting Monday. For information on what to eat and what not to, read the following first. Make sure all your meals are balanced by using these simple guidelines.

Nutritional and Diet Plan Guidelines

Here are the tips that I have collected. Feel free to send your comments and suggestions to me directly by email, or post them on my Facebook page.

Eat less than last week. Rather than eating three meals a day, cut your meals into smaller portions to eat throughout the day. I found myself eating three meals most days and having a snack at around three in the afternoon as well as another one in the evening. Eating smaller but more frequent meals gives me enough food to keep me from feeling hungry, yet I still eat less in total.

Eat breakfast every morning. This is a must. We need to eat a healthy breakfast every morning to perform at our best and feel positive throughout the day. When people skip breakfast, they tend to develop a headache or gastric problems because the last meal they ate was twelve hours before. Remember that eating fruit with a nutritious breakfast will probably save you time and also prevent you from becoming weak and lethargic. In addition, breakfast recharges your brain and your body, and you will be able to perform more efficiently in just about everything you do. Preparing a good breakfast is quick and easy; simply pour low-fat milk over oats. Have a hot cup of tea, but avoid coffee, as most coffee beans are roasted with butter or oil.

Time invested in breakfast is valuable, and skipping meals is linked to obesity.

Nineteen

The Fitness Ladder

If you think you can't do exercises, try doing them. Do not say no. Or consider other simple activities that you can practice in your own time.

An average person can burn many calories in an hour, and it is very simple. You can burn 100 calories per hour by standing, and 80 calories per hour by sleeping. Yes, so go to bed early, sleep for eight hours, and rise early each morning. This is good for your health.

Brisk walking can burn 200 calories per hour and swimming almost 400 calories per hour. As an active tennis player, you can burn up to 450 calories per hour. Jogging helps you to burn more than 600 calories per hour. Always do safe exercises.

My advice is to start with brisk walking, which will help you to burn 90 to 100 calories per hour. However, remember the following.

- A chocolate bar is 500 calories!
- A beef burger is 560 calories!
- A fish burger 380 calories!
- Three slices of pizza are 500 calories!
- A bowl of laksa, an Asian delight made of coconut noodle with vermicelli, is 490 calories!

Before you have a bite, check the label. You might be surprised. Now you understand why even one hour of exercise a day will not count for much if you eat unhealthy meals. Therefore, be alert about what you eat.

Haresh Buxani

Please check with your doctor first before you start on a diet, and your doctor will advise you accordingly.

You can be slimmer and healthier in your mind and your body. Do not make excuses that you can't do it or that you are a failure. Remove the "I can't ..." and replace it with "Yes ... it's possible."

Keep your spirits up, and believe you can do it. It may take six months or a year or two. However, never give up.

Twenty

A Doctor Advises

Our bodies are made up of approximately 75 percent water, and we lose this water by exercising, brisk walking, running, urinating, etc. Think of what you really need in order to survive: is it water, food, or air?

My doctor advised me jokingly that nowadays the younger generation believes that we survive on social networks.

Water plays a major role in your body. Approximately 80 percent of our body is made up of water. Our brain is made up 70 percent water, and our muscle tissue also contains about 75 percent water by weight. Moreover, 90 percent of our blood is also water. Every day, we must drink two liters of liquid, which can be in a form of soup, water, tea, or juices.

What is the best time to drink water?

- 200 milliliters of water when you wake up in the morning

- 200 milliliters of water before taking your shower

- 100 milliliters of tea or coffee with your breakfast

- 200 milliliters of water before you start work

- 200 milliliters of water thirty minutes before lunch

- 200 milliliters of water thirty minutes after lunch

- 100 milliliters of tea or coffee in midafternoon

- 200 milliliters of water in the evening

- 200 milliliters of water 30 minutes before dinner

- 200 milliliters of water 30 minutes after dinner

- 200 milliliters of water before you go to sleep at night

By applying the above method, you will drink two liters of water in one day.

Now tell me, is that difficult to do? I don't think so, and it's healthy to drink water, as it contains zero calories. However, not all people like to drink water, and I am not sure why.

Twenty-One

Important Information

The top three illnesses currently on the rise are cancer, heart attack, and deep vein thrombosis. If you are undergoing cancer treatment or have a heart problem, your doctor will advise you on a diet good for you. This may include instructions to avoid sweets, spicy food, salt, alcohol, and tobacco.

In addition, you may be taking Coumadin or Warfarin as part of your treatment. I am taking Warfarin, which is an anticoagulant (blood thinner) used for deep vein thrombosis and other health issues. Heart patients use it too. Warfarin reduces the formation of blood clots and is used to prevent heart attacks and strokes.

Your Warfarin dosage will be monitored by your doctor; your blood will be checked on a regular basis to make sure that the dose you are taking is right for you. It is important that you do everything you can to help this drug perform properly. This includes avoiding dietary supplements, minerals, and herbs that can interfere with the way in which Warfarin works.

If you are taking this medication, do not start a diet without consulting your doctors first. Eat your normal balanced and healthy meals. It is important *not to go on a weight loss diet or crash diet,* or make other changes to your eating habits.

In addition, while you are taking Warfarin, do not take any new or different dietary supplements or minerals or eat any dark green vegetables or herbs without discussing it with your doctor. These can interfere with the way Warfarin works in your body and may lead to serious complications. Call your doctor immediately if you are unable to eat for several days or if you have diarrhea or a fever. The lack of food decreases the amount of vitamin K in your body and could affect the way Warfarin works. These precautions are important, because the effects of Warfarin depend on the amount of vitamin K in your body.

Now, let me share with you another sickness that had no cure until now: lupus. Patients are suffering from many different types of lupus today, and there are about five million people suffering from lupus globally.

What Is Lupus?

Lupus can affect joints, muscles, and other parts of the body. It is often described as an autoimmune disease. This means that for some unknown reason, people with lupus seem to develop antibodies that usually fight bacteria and viruses but attack healthy tissues instead. This produces inflammation in different parts of the body, resulting in pain and swelling. Lupus can affect the skin, heart, lungs, nervous system, kidneys, and blood—and in particular the immune system. It is a chronic, systemic disease, which means it lasts a long time, probably for the rest of your life. However, nearly all people with lupus have periods of improvement (remissions). Some people have complete and long-lasting remissions.

Who Gets Lupus?

Studies have shown that Indians and Chinese are twice as likely to suffer from lupus than Caucasians. Lupus also has more severe clinical manifestations in Asians than in Caucasians.

What Causes Lupus?

We don't know the cause of lupus. Some people seem to inherit the tendency to get a disease like lupus. Research suggests that an unidentified virus may trigger the disease. A few drugs taken for conditions like high blood pressure or tuberculosis can cause symptoms just like lupus, but these symptoms always disappear when the drug is stopped. Exposure to sunlight seems to trigger lupus in some people.

Lupus Symptoms

Lupus can present in many different ways. The onset is usually gradual, with the development of vague feelings of illness, until specific lupus symptoms develop. Symptoms of lupus vary, but some of the most common ones are

- Fever
- Headache
- Fatigue
- Depression
- Loss of appetite
- Weight loss
- Easy bruising
- Aches and pains
- Edema/swelling
- Hair loss
- Swollen glands

The following symptoms and signs are much more suggestive of lupus:

- A rash over the cheeks and bridge of the nose
- Rashes after exposure to the sun or ultraviolet light
- Ulcers inside the mouth
- Arthritis of two or more joints

- Pleurisy (pain in the chest on deep breathing)
- Seizures
- Anemia
- Raynaud's disease (fingers turn white and/or blue in the cold)

Diagnosing Lupus

Lupus is easy to diagnose when an individual has many of the characteristic symptoms and signs, but is made more difficult if only a few are present. Laboratory tests are usually conducted to help confirm or reject the diagnosis. These tests may include a blood count and urine analysis. More specific laboratory tests look for antibodies—in particular, antibodies to the nuclei of cells (the antinuclear antibodies test) and antibodies to DNA. Over 99 percent of people with lupus have a positive ANA test. However, only about 30 percent of people with a positive ANA test have lupus.

Treatment

Lupus is an unpredictable disease, but in most cases it can be successfully treated. Once an effective treatment program has been started, it is important for the patient to keep to it faithfully and to inform the doctor of any change in symptoms so that the medications can be modified.

Medications for Lupus

Corticosteroids.

Prednisolone is the most commonly used drug. Steroids are powerful drugs that suppress inflammations and are commonly used in controlling lupus. It is important for the patient to keep to the prescribed dose. Flare-ups of the disease can occur if the dose is reduced too rapidly. *Never alter your dosage of corticosteroids without first discussing it with your doctor, since stopping them or changing the dosage can quickly make you very ill.*

Antimalarial drugs.

These seem to be effective in reducing inflammation and controlling skin problems. They also decrease reactions to sun exposure.

Aspirin and other anti-inflammatory drugs.

Aspirin and other anti-inflammatory drugs, such as Indocid, Clinoril, Brufen, and Naproxen, may be the only medications a doctor will prescribe. These drugs control pain and reduce inflammation.

Immunosuppressive drugs.

Immunosuppressive drugs are usually used in conjunction with corticosteroids to control more severe cases. If you're taking an immunosuppressive, regular blood tests will be done, because the drug can interfere with the formation of blood cells.

Ointments and skin creams.

Your doctor may prescribe a cream containing a sunscreen to protect against damage from the sun. Corticosteroids containing creams are used to control skin rashes.

Pregnancy and Lupus

Pregnancy can mean special problems for women with lupus. Although the majority have normal pregnancies, there is an increased risk of early marriage. There may be a worsening of symptoms after delivery. It is important for the patient and doctor to discuss and plan the best time for the patient to have a child.

Coping with Lupus

In a chronic disease like lupus, social and emotional problems are common. You may experience feelings of anger, fear, and depression. It is extremely helpful to be able to talk about how you feel with someone close to you or someone who has had similar problems.

Exercising and finding ways to relax may make it easier for you to cope. A good support system can also help. This may include family, friends, support groups, or doctors. Besides providing support, a support group can make you feel better about yourself and help you to maintain a good outlook.

Lupus Association (Singapore)

The Lupus Association (Singapore) is a self-help group dedicated to providing support for patients and their families. The group aims to assist lupus patients by providing practical support and by giving people the opportunity to share their experiences with others who have lupus. The Lupus Association (Singapore) is committed to researching the disease and improving understanding of the disease, especially among people with lupus and their families.

(The material for "What Is Lupus" was taken from the website of Lupus Association (Singapore). For more information on Systemic Lupus Erythematosus (SLE, or Lupus), visit their website: http://e-lupus.org. International enquiries, please contact by email: enquiry@e-lupus. org. Please "like" their Facebook page: https://www.facebook.com/ lupusassociationsg.)

How Is Lupus Treated?

You may need special kinds of doctors to treat the many symptoms of lupus. Your health care team may include the following:

- A family doctor
- Rheumatologists: doctors who treat arthritis and autoimmune diseases
- Nephrologists: doctors who treat kidney disease

- Hematologists: doctors who treat blood disorders
- Dermatologists: doctors who treat skin diseases
- Neurologists: doctors who treat problems with the nervous system
- Cardiologists: doctors who treat heart and blood vessel problems
- Endocrinologists: doctors who treat problems related to the glands and hormones
- Nurses
- Psychologists

Your family doctor will develop a treatment plan to fit your needs. He or she should review the plan often to be sure it's working. You should report new symptoms to your doctor right away so that treatment can be changed if needed.
The goals of a treatment plan might include

- preventing flare-ups,
- treating flare-ups when they occur, and
- reducing organ damage and other problems.

Change of Lifestyle

Lifestyle changes are needed to reduce the incidence of relapse.

- Avoid sun bathing.
- Avoid sun entirely when it is strongest: 11 a.m. to 5 p.m.
- Use sunblock cream on your face and hands.
- Wear protective clothing.
- Get regular exercise, but do not overdo.
- Drink about 1.5 to 2 liters of water daily.
- Remember to eat healthy meals.
- Avoid alcohol intake, and do not smoke.
- Sleep at least eight hours every night.

Commit Yourself to the Following

- Consume three healthy meals and three healthy snacks every day.

- Plan your diet, and always have fresh and low-fat food in stock.

- Keep it simple. Do not get caught up in the specifics of your diet. Start simply by just counting calories.

- Chew your food slowly and chat more with your friends or loved ones during meals.

- Make healthier food selections like fruits, vegetables, whole-grain cereals and beans, low-fat or nonfat dairy products, low-fat meat, fish, and skinless poultry.

- Avoid food that is oily and high in fat and calories.

- Avoid food that is high in sugar, and eliminate pastries, candy bars, and pies.

- Eat a variety of fruits and vegetables.

- Start by eating five servings of fruits and vegetables every single day.

- Stay simple and stay healthy, and almost any sickness will be more under control.

Just think,
we live on earth only once.

Now is the time to start taking your baby steps
and to take up the challenge to become a new you.

In life, there are many things that we can control,
but the two things we can't control are our birth and death.

These two matters are not in our hands,
but you can manifest everything else.
Do not delay. Start your engine today.

Twenty-Two

Hunger for Success

Have you written down your desires, listing them from one to ten? If you have not yet, stop reading this book, and get your pencil and paper out. Think of your desires and wishes, and write them down.

You have now started wishing, and this affirmation list is for your eyes only. Nobody should see it, so you can even write down your most secret ideas to look at every day. Add bright ideas and dreams when they come to mind. You can also post notes of your dreams anywhere you wish, so you can see them every day. Or design a wall in your home or office to post your desires on. You will then see and be able to visualize them. Then watch your miracles come true in one to five years.

Complete this affirmations list by tonight or the end of this week. Remember to write down your abundance affirmation and believe that this is possible. Use your thoughts carefully and positively, seeing the picture repeatedly in your mind. Imagine it being surrounded by positive energy, and feel the positive vibrations. Visualize every day what you want from your life. If possible, say it loudly three times or more so that your words can be heard by the universe.

Do not lack planning, and do not lack trust. If you think that you lack something, this will not work for you, and you will be disappointed with your affirmation list. Remove negativity from your mind and your life. Focus only on positive thoughts, and believe them.

I know you can be a success. You will then feel proud of yourself for overcoming obstacles. Focus on your positive goals, and you will definitely be happy one day. You will feel great for being a successful person who has achieved abundance and prosperity.

Begin your road to success now. Do not give up easily. If you fail, try again and again.

Twenty-Three

What Is Prosperity?

For me, my family come first, love comes second, investments third, friends fourth, and luxuries last. In addition, I love helping friends and strangers by giving free advice on success and many other positive things.

Saving is also very important. I do not spend much, and I do not believe in getting rich quickly through multilevel marketing or lotteries, as I know the only one who wins is the one who owns the game; the odds are usually not on my side.

Say, for instance, you have a good career with a firm, and your salary goes into your personal bank account. To save money, open a savings account, and inform your bank that from now on, 10 percent (or 20 or whatever you prefer) of your salary is to be transferred into that account. Do not apply for an ATM card for this new saving account. Keep it open, and update it every year. From then on, do not withdraw any money from it, as you do not want to jeopardize your special investment plan.

What can the 10 percent or 20 percent of your salary do? It is a small amount, but when you check your account balance after two years, five years, and ten years, you will see just how rich you will be after saving your money for twenty years.

Twenty-Four

Dream for What You Want

Nowadays, almost everyone has a home or two. If you don't have a property of your own, not to worry. Do not give up, as property prices this year (2014 and 2015) are the highest ever in Asia. Remember that there is a recession every six years, and the downturn in Asia might be in the year 2020, but many top property investors are expecting it in 2016 to 2017. Buy your own residential real estate or other property at that time. Purchase a property at a good location. Wait for the right time: when you have saved enough money in your personal bank account. Start small and start tomorrow.

Moreover, if you live outside Asia, the best time to buy your own property in the United States and the United Kingdom is right now (2014 and 2015), as the price of real estate is fairly low. Invest, and see how prices climb up again. I know that one day you will own a real estate or a joint-venture property. Trust me, you will.

Property investment is a good long-term holding as inflation is rising. Every time you buy real estate in your hometown or in other countries with a 20 percent to 25 percent down payment, you borrow the balance from a bank or finance company and pay the loan off over twenty or twenty-five years.

Every property you purchase must be bought at the right time: when the property market is low or while the economy is in a recession, you only need to hold on to it for three or five years or more. You will definitely make a profit if you hold onto it for as long as possible. You can buy and sell property within a month, but try not to sell your own home, the one in which you live. This is where your family members are living. If you are upgrading from a smaller home to a bigger home, that is fine. You can wait for the right time to buy a new home, such as when the interest rate is low. Buy, but buy real estate at a prime location only. If you have an extra property and can afford to play the game of buying and selling, do it.

Search for the property you need and create a powerful, inspirational true story of your own.

In addition, guide your children in how to invest. Yes, you, as a parent, need to teach your kids about money, saving, life, and how to be long-term investors in order to earn good yields. Start today and guide your children from as young as possible. It will benefit them.

But first *you* need to be an investor.

Twenty-Five

Compound Investing

You could be employed or unemployed, or you could be a compound investor. Either way, guide your kids in using money, such as by playing money games that impart an understanding of cost factors and how to save. Open a new bank account for each of them so that they too learn what saving is. Saving money is good for all ages.

Why do people wake up every morning and rush to work? The reason is simple: to make more money. People tend to save 10 percent to 20 percent of their monthly income and use the balance to pay their monthly bills.

There are many ways to create wealth. Some go for fast money, and some work hard for theirs. Some earn their money from high-yielding stocks, while others keep money in the bank and earn interest on it. Some high-net-worth individuals live a life of luxury, spending on their needs and wants, and some real estate investors earn their money by holding onto their property for many years as investments.

Guide your kids in compound savings, teaching them the right way and what it can do for them.

Go to the chapters title "What Is a Blueprint?" (Parts 1, 2, and 3) to learn what a compound investor is.

Twenty-Six

Create Your Own Life

Y ou need to create a powerful, inspirational true story of your own. Never give up on life. As long as your heart beats, you are young at heart. Even when you reach the age of forty-six or seventy-six, you are still young at heart. Think positively and write in your journal. Create and record your daily affirmation list, and revise it every day. Go out and buy yourself a new outfit. And when was the last time you went on a good, long holiday?

Do not wait any longer. Use a bookmark to keep your place, and close this book. Get your newspaper and flip through to the Travel section. Choose a place where you would like to go on holiday. Circle the article, call the travel agency, ask for the best price for the trip, and pre-book it. Share your good news about your vacation trip *tonight* at the dinner table or with friends.

Then come back to my book and continue reading.

My favorite quote is, "Don't ask what the world needs. Ask what makes you come alive, and go and do it. It is possible because what the world needs is people who have come alive."

The difference between school and real life is that in school we are taught a lesson by our teachers and then take a test. In real life, we are given tests that teach us lessons in how to survive on our own and be successful. You can also find a mentor, watch what he or she does, and follow suit. But you will not create anything of your own this way. I want you to create something of your own: a signature and lifestyle that you can be proud.

We have been trained to survive and to be creative thinkers in taking care of our loved ones; we are expected to earn an income to support ourselves and our loved ones. Look ahead. We need to dream of a positive life. We need to figure out what we want in life as we live in a magical place. If we want our dreams to come true, what should we do first, and how can we make them come true?

If you have a life of luxury, good for you. But if you are living in a moderate way, how do you make your dream come true? We need to see the results in our mind in order for us to dream about how to go about achieving them. Our mind is a very powerful tool that can work for us. We are the producers of our thoughts. Thoughts become words. Words become success.

For example, the vision we have now is of the newest smartphone, the newest tablet, and all the other new digital devices. We are surrounded by abundance in this beautiful world. We are living in the universe. We do not know how or where we are going, and we are always there on time, as we always think of the result. So, take your baby steps and allow your dreams to come true.

Take action now. Be an inspiring person.

In the end, you will be fulfilled. Keep all your possibilities open, broaden your mind, respect your elders and your ancestors, and be a spiritual person. You need to find out who you really are.

Twenty-Seven

Remind Yourself That Your Life Begins Now

Let me tell you about my life. I was a dropout at the age of seventeen due to my father being unwell. As I was the eldest son, my parents suggested that I start working in a relative's shop, and I started saving for my future then. I moved out of my family's house and went to work in a new city, and I began a new life. I worked as a salesperson in a retail store for almost thirteen years.

During the first three years, I took one day off to visit my parents. Thereafter, the company expanded by opening many branches. During the next ten years, the only days I took off were the four days a year when the shopping center was closed for a special holiday.

After having worked from 10 a.m. to 11 p.m. daily, 361 days a year for thirteen years, I decided to pull up the hand brake and move back to my hometown. Four years later, I slowly upgraded myself by going into a joint venture with my family. At that time, my younger brother, who was enjoying a wonderful career, decided we would both become commercial property investors. Back in the day, we were called businessmen. Today, by chance, I have become an author.

I dreamed about being an author some years ago, but I did not believe my dream could come true. I started writing this book by typing a page per week. If I had said that I needed to do this or that I needed to become the author of a book, I might not have succeeded, and I might not have reached this point if I had not taken baby steps. I wrote a page on alternate days from 2008 until 2014. Would you believe it?

When this book was almost 99 percent complete, I was required to get the permission of two authors whose quotes I had used. I will be successful when launching this one day; I have a magical feeling inside of me about it.

Will this book be a success? I am not sure, but I feel positive about it, as what I shared about baby steps has always worked for me. I hope it would work for you as well.

If you are born poor, it's not your fault.
But if you die poor,
it's definitely your fault.

***

What is next?

You need to be transformed and to begin
to practice what you have learned so far.
Enjoy this moment of greatness:
"One day, I will be successful."

You need to be
hungry for prosperity and for success.

Only then will it work for you.

Twenty-Eight

How I Changed My Life

Some of my friends once asked me what difference it would make if I didn't do the Eight Minutes Practice.

First, I must say that the Eight Minutes Practice had a tremendous impact on me. My life has changed, and let me tell you how. I was once only 10 percent positive and had no expectations. Everything was easy for me, as my family supported my lifestyle. I was breezing through life. I was a cheerful person, respected, friendly, loyal, and humble. I sometimes felt great joy, though there were days when I was unhappy about the obstacles in my life. I blamed my luck and complained a lot, always feeling like the victim and blaming others for my misery due to my unhappy marriages. This was because I was always thinking negatively. In addition, my right leg had been amputated from above the knee in 2008. I had doctors all around me, telling my family and me how seriously sick I was. I also became depressed.

I didn't enjoy reading books, as I was not a bookworm. However, after watching positive movies and practicing the One Day Method, I saw 30 percent improvement instantly. I now go to bookshops and spend an hour or two browsing through motivational books, and I buy a few and read them. Having looked forward to success and being fortunate, I really believed I could make it happen, but it did not. I failed again.

I tried again and again. I kept repeating that I would never give up, ever. I built positive energy within me. That took longer to do than expected, but I never gave up. Initially, it was very hard to be completely positive, but I still did not give up. I wanted to change myself by building a positive character within me.

One day, I just could not believe it. I had already achieved 90 percent of what I had hoped in changing myself. But I was not sure what was I supposed to do next, which road I was meant to walk, as I had been given everything in life. I was a golden spoon boy, but something felt strange. There was something missing.

Fear built up within me as I questioned whether I would be successful. My close friend said there was a secret in the book and told me to read it carefully. It took me years to understand what the secret was and how I could change or improve myself.

I analyzed myself again and again carefully and often. I started understanding how our mind works. Then I asked myself, *what do I really want?*

Twenty-Nine

What Do You Need to Do for Eight Minutes?

Continue to bring abundance and prosperity into your life. How? You need to practice it every day—for only eight minutes. You need to change your understanding. Change your thoughts, and focus on what you really want in life.

Abundance and prosperity have a close relationship. By believing in yourself and changing your thoughts, you can change your life. I can definitely predict your future and say that you will live a better life and enjoy the greater things in life. But to get there, you need to do this Eight Minute Practice.

- *Do your morning warm-up for eight minutes every day.*

- *Do your exercises three times per week for eight minutes only.*

- *Read your wish list every day for eight minutes only.*

Keep your wish list card in your pocket. Whenever you feel like reading it, do so for eight minutes. Keep doing it every day. Slowly, after a few months, you will feel the changes within you. Your life, career, marriage, and dreams will soon be manifested as you have already sent your signal to the universe.

Read your card every day. This will definitely create good energies for you whenever you feel you are going off track or are feeling miserable. Read the card and turn your negative thoughts into positive ones. One thing you must remember is this:

Thoughts Becoming Affirmations = Success

When you feel the success within you, go out and buy yourself some new clothes and new shoes. You do not need to buy high-end clothing. Buy something you can afford, and see the difference within you, as you will be a new person.

You will have changed your life, and that will make you feel different. To be a successful person, you need to create a blueprint for yourself for the weeks ahead.

Thirty

What Is a Blueprint? (Part 1)

You can't work in the same job for twenty years, can you? I worked for thirteen years on the minimum salary. You could be earning the same low salary, but you can't do that. No, you can't!

Every two or three years, try to think of something new, of how to improve yourself and create a new blueprint for yourself. Nowadays, we have been overtaken by the digital world, and everyone is busy communicating on their mobile phones and the Internet. Find something to do that could create a higher vision for yourself than that, so that with your blueprint, you can achieve a new and higher level of income or investments. Find a way to double your brainpower so that you can create a new blueprint.

Think about what I have just said. Give yourself a five-minute break from this book, go and get yourself a cup of tea or a drink, and come back to read, as I am now going to guide you.

Based on my experience and a current experiment with my future expectations, I can tell you there are many untapped potentials for you as you look for something worthwhile to do—something new. I know it is not easy to make goals, but if your heart and mind are aligned, you may find what you have been searching all the while.

Back in the day, our parents used to tell us to study and work hard in order to achieve our goals and to try not to do anything wrong—then we would reach our goals. They discouraged their own children from thinking creatively and dreaming, as they did not believe that dreams could come true. Some parents overruled their teenage children's desires by telling them not to touch this and not to smell that. So those children did not know how to create anything. They felt that if their parents did not approve, they could not act. Therefore, the children blocked their minds and followed what their parents told them to do.

However, we are living in a new digital world today, and it is a totally different world. Today we use our minds more than our hands. How we create an opportunity for tomorrow is all in our mind. People born into this new world are doing their own brainstorming and are far more creative than ever before. They also have much more freedom than ever before to be so. People nowadays use more imagination, visualization, and brainstorming. People ask me a lot of questions about creativity, and my answer is usually the same: daydream, as it transforms your dreams into reality. Thoughts become words, and words become affirmations leading you to success; so go ahead and dream.

The wonderful part of creativity is that everyone has it. Every one of us can tap the unconscious mind so much faster than before. We can improve the quality of our minds and move faster in doing anything we want to do in this world in which we live.

Thirty-One

What Is a Blueprint? (Part 2)

Human beings are like computers. We can load the most important data into our minds and create new opportunities instantly. We have the universe supporting us in whatever we do. When we use the new digital mobile devices and computer, we are actually improving our quality of life. We can innovate. How I wish we'd had this ability long before now. But it is not too late.

Everyone had fresh ideas come to him or her. Try your idea, since you have nothing to lose. Creativity is a way of improving your life, and we are creative individuals. We can store all the good things in our minds, such as what we see or read, and we have the ability to solve any problem.

Start working on your challenges and think of your possibilities. *You* can create a new blueprint for yourself.

Practice the One Day Method. Read the affirmation list that you have created. Read it for only eight minutes. Find the secrets to retiring rich.

Let me share more on the idea of a blueprint, about how you can go from what you have now to what you will need to live well. Some of my friends think you need to be earning a five-figure income and stash away thousands of dollars a month just to retire rich. Think again: is this right?

I can show you how I saved every cent I could and saved dollars in my savings account at the same time. Furthermore, I took half of my savings out to make my first investment, which was with my family.

You, too, could do the same and see for yourself how rich you will become one day.

I was only seventeen years old when I dropped out of school, as my dad was ill. While other boys were in school getting good grades, I worked and earned ten dollars a day. Every day, I saved five dollars and spent only five. Some of my friends and distant relatives found out that I had been saving five dollars per day, and they mocked me. They ask what I could get for US$150.00 a month and told me I was just wasting my time. It would be better to go out and spent the US$150.00 on a dinner every month.

At that point, my imagined mentor was Donald Trump. I wanted to be like him. I knew that I could not have been now, but I always imagined I could. I just wished I could. Therefore, my focus on saving was genuine.

If you have not saved a single cent toward retirement, I can show you how.

Thirty-Two

What Is a Blueprint? (Part 3)

In the next eight minutes, you will know how to pump up your portfolio and have extra cash in your saving account. You will discover a simple technique to help you fulfill your retirement plan, and so much more. Even if you are fifty-five years old now, you can still do it. For example, if your income is approximately US$1,000.00 per month, and you take 10 percent from that amount and start saving US$100.00 on a monthly basis, with an average yearly interest rate of 1.5 percent, you will have approximately US$24,360.00 in twenty years. You must remember, too, that there is inflation.

Another example: Every time your savings reach US$5,000.00, transfer this money into a fixed deposit account to earn a higher interest rate. The longer you hold onto it, the higher it will appreciate. Then you can watch your money multiply for you even when you are asleep at night.

You might be wondering what this amount could do for you. Let me give you another scenario. Be a compound investor and see for yourself the magic that could happen. Let's say you are twenty-five years old, and you are saving almost nothing. You then start saving on a monthly basis. After thirty years, when you celebrate your fifty-fifth birthday, you will have saved US$416,171.00 in your fixed deposit account at the bank. If you had saved the normal way, you would have earned only US$139,929.00 in today's dollar with an average yearly inflation rate.

Where did all that money come from?

Well, it came from your humble savings of US$200.00 each month, which you set aside for your compound savings. Plus, you received cash gifts on special occasions. Not withdrawing any money from that account caused the savings to multiply to a huge amount for your retirement.

You have become a compound investor. When you had no full-time job a long time ago, you started saving US$200.00 whenever you made the money from your part-time work. You need to save to compound interest for the long term.

Now you know how to be an investor by beginning to invest in a small way, ranging from five dollars to US$200.00 in a bank account that pays a yearly interest rate. Do it, and you'll see how mind-blowing it is to become a compound investor. It is magical feeling.

Another solution is putting your savings in high-yield stocks that give you 4 to 7 percent out of your preferred stock. You might be adding to your pocket much more than your yearly income. Amazing, is it not?

Thirty-Three

Remember the Six Golden Rules

The key to multiplying prosperity, harmony, and happiness is in your hands with these six rules:

1. Create your destiny. Love your career first, and then join the flow.

2. When you love what you do, universal happiness enters your life.

3. You do not go to work for money, for if you do that, it means that you are not happy.

4. If you love what you do, your work will generate your energy, no matter what you do, and 10 percent will be the savings growth just for you. However, that is only if you can discipline yourself to take out that 10 percent of your monthly income and spend only 90 percent.

5. From here, your saving is continuing no matter what. You have two choices. Make the right one, because if you do, you will know how good it feels to be saving this way. And this is the only way.

6. Your gut feeling will tell you in the next thirty days that the choice you have made is indeed the right one.

Be your own investor. That is all you need to manifest your dream.

Feel the Power

Discover a new you.

Just follow the baby steps, and take one step at a time.
Remember, if you have a fear, turn it into your friend.
Yes, make your fear your best friend.
Go for it and be a dreamer.
You are a creator.
It's possible.

* *

Let me trust the path I'm on
not because I can see where the open doors are,
but because You are with me.

Edward Seah

Thirty-Four

How to Be Fearless and Have No Anger

The most important thing you need to know is how to eliminate fear and anger.

Try to get to know your closest friend: Mr. or Ms. Fear. Do not be afraid of inviting him or her closer to make him or her your best friend. If you can achieve that, I am sure you will not have any problems with your next step in becoming a successful person, as you have broken the barriers in your journey.

Enjoy success in everything you do. Believe me, and believe in yourself. "Fear is only your shadow." Remember that. Make Mr. or Ms. Fear your best friend. Always do the task that you fear the most, and the rest will become easy. Try it, and you will know. If you are not sure how to do it, let me explain.

You have to learn to control fear and anger yourself, which takes time. No one can change you but yourself. When you are in fear, people tend to bully you. People take advantage of your weakness and try to dominate you. People may give you a meal and encourage you to eat more, and then they'll tell you that you are not eating properly, which may lead to you gaining weight. People encourage you to watch old movies that bring happiness, sadness, hate, fear, and delight. These emotions take you back to your past, and history might repeat itself, because as you sleep, your mind may return to the old ways instead of remaining in the frame of mind in which you were before you watched those movies.

When you awake the next day, you may feel the anger that you felt in the past. Your feelings at that moment are as they were after watching the movie. That is how some people become depressed. Old movies can bring the past into the present.

There are people who have a strong mind and can control their emotions, but there are some who can't, because they carry heavy baggage. That is why you need to remove your old fears and not allow them to build up. That is why I say to treat fear as your best buddy. When you watch the old movies, nothing will happen to you, because you will be able to laugh at yourself.

Do you know why? Because fear is now your best friend, and you have forgiven the person whom you hate the most. You have released your anger from your mind and your heart. You now feel more relaxed. Moreover, with a calm mind-set, you can now control your anger and fear.

Heal yourself by doing a thirty-minute prayer or meditation, thanking God for what you have and asking God for the three principles. You ask … you must believe … and you will receive. Believe that you can achieve things in life and take good care of your body and your soul, as your body is your temple. Always give thanks to God for your success, happiness, prosperity, and loving family, and pray for your children to have a good future.

Before you go to sleep, read your affirmation list. Update it daily, and watch your life improve in the next thirty days. Fear and anger are now your best friends.

No and *yes* are two short words that need much thought.
We missed many things because we said no too early and yes too late.

Unknown

Thirty-Five

The Five Secrets of Successful Relationships

By believing in yourself, you can change your life just by changing your thoughts. You can predict your own future and believe that you will live a better life—and trust me, you will. Come, read the extraordinary recipe of a successful relationship below. You are about to build a foundation that can withstand any storm, and I mean *any*!

But first we must understand something. Most marital relationships break down because of a lack of understanding or a lack of money. This is where depression enters a marriage, where arguments come into the relationship, where tempers flare, and so on. In any relationship, people encounter difficulties, a lack of understanding, challenges, and negativity. But in the real world, we seldom learn that the most important thing needed in a relationship is trust.

Building a relationship and laying the foundation stones will bring out the best in the relationship. Let me give you a few pointers, and you can take over from there.

Secret Number One: For any relationship to work, you must know who you are and what you want in life. Some want their partner to take care of them, and some want a soul mate; some want a friend with whom they can talk. However, the most important is to know how your future partner behaves toward your parents, and the respect that he or she shows to them, as well as the good behavior and the values he or she has. Those who know how to respect their parents-in-law know how to respect you.

Secret Number Two: Do not keep choosing the wrong person as your life partner. Go to different places to find yourself a partner, and do not pretend to be someone you are not. Do not give up on life too quickly, as life is meaningful. Cherish every moment.

Secret Number Three: Do not try to change your life partner. Just let your partner be who he or she is. Many want to change their partner. This is not a relationship; it's manipulation. I believe that if the person loves you and cares for you, he or she will love you the way you are. If someone feels accepted, he or she may change himself or herself.

Secret Number Four: We must learn the difference between real and fake love. With real love, you feel excited. You get good energy within you and feel attached. Fake love makes you happy for a couple of months, and then you realize that it is not true love. You feel that something is not right. Maybe your partner starts demanding more money and more gifts, and you begin to spend more and draw more from your monthly income. You receive less love, and your parents are not treated with respect. It is high time to find a new partner.

Secret Number Five: Look for the best in others and yourself. When we focus on the good in others, we see our relationship grow in a healthy manner. The better others feel about you, the better you feel about your partner. Negativity dissolves and positivity grows. You and your partner come together to learn the true meaning of *relationship*, which is to enjoy growth together naturally. Do not think about the past and its failures. Think only on the now. Do not try to control others. Realize that if the person is meant to be with you, he or she will stay, and that will be the greatest relationship ever.

Lastly, discuss your financial situation before you enter into marriage. That is where you can see the true colors of your future partner. It is similar to dipping a tea bag in hot water. The more you dip, the more visible the color becomes.

Once you have followed these five simple secrets, practice building a foundation together. These secrets can turn nothing into something, and you and your partner will remain happy together.

Relationships are available everywhere in abundance, but you have to choose your partner wisely. You know who you are and the type of person with whom you want to spend your life.

Enjoy the honesty, the communication, and the companionship. Enjoy finding the right partner.

Life does not need to be perfect
for us to enjoy a wonderful day.

Thirty-Six

Is Life Important to Us?

Yes, life is important to us. Why is that so? Because we have only one chance to do anything, as we are in a body that can go anywhere to see wonderful places and to enjoy amazing and delicious food.

You only live once, so whatever good you can do, do it now. Whatever advice or help you can give to others, give it now. Do you know why? Life is a once-in-a-lifetime experience. So if you and your family do not know how to appreciate what life is all about, you will miss out on a lot. Create your affirmation list, start your remarkable journey, and see what life is all about.

God created us to appreciate life in love and harmony. Create for yourself a meaningful life. Create happiness within your family and your working life. Try to be hardworking. Serve God with your mind and body by engaging in volunteer work that you enjoy.

Do not take life for granted or live the life you were born into. Rather, create a signature of your own, and live with the dignity you deserve. Life so that everyone remembers you for a long time. Do not do harm to anyone. Show respect to all, and greet your opponents with respect.

Do something good, and share your prestige and friendly environment with your friends and neighbors. Remove all hate and negativity from your mind. Change it into positive thinking, and never regret your past. Life is about learning from our mistakes, as without mistakes, no one ever really learns how to live.

Cherish your life, as you have been given this life only once. Understand the meaning of life, and understand what is good for you.

Discover a new meaning of life, as most people know that the purpose of life is to serve God.

Live life to the fullest. Walk different paths and making the right decisions. You and I will make some mistakes, but we will learn from them and grow stronger.

Understand the Universe and the world you live in.

God bless you.

Logic will get you from A to B.
Imagination will take you everywhere.

Albert Einstein

Thirty-Seven

One Day

W hile in the hospital bed, I wrote down on a piece of paper what I would do "one day." I prayed to God and remained patient and calm. I did not allow the pain, anguish, and anger sully my thinking. I also wrote my affirmation list and kept adding to it:

1) One day, I will be slim.

2) One day, I will be walking.

3) One day, I will take brisk walks.

4) One day, I will run.

5) One day, I will do wall climbing.

6) One day, I will learn to drive again.

7) One day, I will ride on the Singapore cable car.

8) One day, I will take the escalator.

9) One day, I will drive a red Cabriolet.

10) One day, I will ride a bicycle on the beach.

11) One day, I will write my first book.

12) One day, I will achieve financial goals.

13) One day, I will have a girlfriend.

14) One day, I will walk a half-marathon.

15) One day …

What are your affirmations? Write them down.

Thirty-Eight

Your Affirmation List

This is for you if you haven't done your affirmation list yet.

This page will make it easier for you. Just sit down and relax, and imagine what you really want and what you would like to be. Then write your ten wishes below.

1. _____

2. _____

3. _____

4. _____

5. _____

6. _____

7. _____

8. _____

9. _____

10. _____

You will be glad you did this. And you will see how you progress from here.

Thirty-Nine

Choose One Idea—And Go for It!

At this point, look at your list every night before you go to sleep. Choose one idea from the list that you could easily achieve, and pray for your dream to come true. My suggestion is that you trust your intuition on this one idea of yours.

Think of the results and visualize your idea, or take a picture of it and look at it every day. Imagine that you are already successful. What is the next step you need to take?

You may get an idea about something, but your heart may point you in another direction. Sleep on it, and when you wake up, follow your first thought of the day. Think of the four corners: first the possibilities, then the weaknesses, then how successful you will become from making the right decisions—and then go for it. You are about to do something magical, something that will go way beyond where you are at this moment.

If you still have not written down your ten affirmations, and if you still have fear, decide either to live with it or let it go. The choice is yours.

In life, everyone goes though experiences that help you grow, which can sometime be painful or horrible. Whatever it is, you need to decide to let go and move forward or to hang onto fear. I can't help you with what happened to you in the past. What I can do is this: when you come to visit me on the day I launch my book, I will bless you with a big handshake and guide you to move on.

Do not worry about the affirmation list.

Take your time and do it when you feel ready and comfortable. Also consider reading the book twice to understand it fully before starting your baby steps.

Life is short.

Take action now, and learn how to be a successful person.

Forty

Do You Know Yourself Better?

When you find your "soul purpose" in life, is it fate or chance?

Knowing your purpose and pursuing it is the key to success and fulfillment. But it is not that simple. It will take you 120 days to create a mind exercise that digs deep into your subconscious mind, unearthing hidden truths and identifying your soul purpose.

Once you find your soul purpose, how do you get there from here?

- Use your affirmation list or some other compass that helps you to make choices.

- Practice a creative mind exercise that helps you to identify the core values that will guide you throughout your life. Do this, and you will be able to make important decisions that will make it a whole lot easier for you to start your remarkable journey.

- Think about the kind of house you will live in, of the countries to which you will travel, or of something else you want. What does your house look like? Who will you meet? Be a leader and follow your new mind as your brain takes you through this visualization exercise to help you to have a vision of your perfect life.

You have the *magic* in your hands to accomplish these for yourself, but do not forget to dream big!

Go back to your roots and evaluate your progress. Get a pencil and paper, and write down your thoughts. Think. Go back and actually analyze your past, looking for potential drawbacks. Remember that every individual's past is unique. Think of your greatest accomplishment and write it down in the form of a quotation.

Over the next few months, you will be looking at different psychological factors. But first and foremost, you need to start with anxiety. Therefore, jump-start your mind and see the miracle coming to you in the near future.

Being aware of anxiety is important for your own good. Write down some of your successful experiments based on an anxiety analysis. Do not delay; get started on the destiny of your new life. Start innovating and progressing.

You are miserable because you forget the things
you should remember and remember
the things you should forget.

Sally Mok

Forty-One

What Is Anxiety?

People do not recognize their anxiety for what it is. They think there is something wrong with them, so they do not learn how to manage it.

Anxiety is a common and normal experience that can be managed. The first step is to understand and recognize it. Self-awareness is the first step to improvement.

Many people experience anxiety. It is normal to feel anxious when you are entering the fulfillment of a new vision, such as having an interview or becoming a compound investor. Anxiety motivates us to prepare for the job interview or to focus on our new journey.

When your body feels tight; when you sweat or feel dizzy, have an upset stomach, or feel pain in your chest pain, it may be due to illness, but it rarely is. Often it is anxiety. When you are being interviewed for a job, planning to be an investor, or walking into your new creative dream, it will likely feel uncomfortable.

You may get upset with people easily or enter into arguments for no apparent reason, and on some days, you might have a hard time thinking clearly. This can become so overwhelming that you want to avoid doing anything. Because of this, most people stop doing what they want to do.

What is really happening to you and your body when you feel anxious? Basically, your muscles tense up as your body prepares for danger; it shuts down the internal systems that are needed for long-term survival.

For example, digestion is not needed in times of danger. Because of this, anxiety may lead to stomach upset, dizziness, or sweating. You may also feel yourself breathing quickly. When your body is preparing for action, it makes sure there is enough blood and oxygen circulating to your major muscles and organs, allowing you to fight off the danger.

Remember, anxiety is not dangerous or harmful. All the sensations you feel when you are anxious are basically to protect you from danger. Anxiety triggers your body to react to the feeling of insecurity, but there is no real danger.

Rather than trying to eliminate anxiety, we need to bring the anxiety level down to a manageable point so we can focus on our new vision. Seek help if you think you have a serious anxiety disorder. If you don't, there are still number of things you can do on your own to deal with your anxiety better.

- Practice muscle relaxation. For example, do a simple meditation for thirty minutes and do a breathing exercise at the same time, or try to rest more in bed. Drink more fluids to help your muscles relaxed.

- Do not breathe faster when you are anxious, because when you do that, you are likely to sweat and feel nauseated, causing you to be even more anxious. Try calm breathing. This means inhaling and exhaling at a slow and gentle pace. Inhale through your nose, hold your breath for a second, and exhale through your mouth. Do this for ten to fifteen minutes, and you will be fine.

- Some people tend to see the world as threatening. Their thinking can thus be overly negative and sometimes unrealistic, which can trigger anxiety and also slow down recovery. These thoughts can sometimes take over your mind and your heart. One way to manage this is to think of a balanced life, which will allow you to see things more clearly. However, it takes time to align your thinking, so keep practicing, have patience, and try to think in a realistic way.

- Make fear your best friend. Believe me and believe in yourself. Remember that fear is only your shadow. Make Mr. or Ms. Fear your best friend.

Now you know how to manage your anxiety. It might take a long time to heal yourself, but do not give up. Take time to reward yourself. You need to keep positive habits and ignore the negative. Think positively always. That is the essence of the One Day Method and the baby steps.

Always remember, you need to bring your anxiety down to a manageable level, so that you can focus on your new vision of life. Remember, anxiety is normal, and it is not dangerous at all. Everyone experiences it, and you can turn it into a kind of successful anxiety. It can create a new creative life and a dream that will benefit you.

You will not be able to create anything of your own if you think in an unrealistic way and if you hang on to negativity and fear. I want you to create something of your own, something unique, and to enjoy the new lifestyle that is waiting only for you.

Then you can be proud of yourself for achieving results.

Do not give up
too soon in life.

Forty-Two

Jump-Start Your Brain

Here is another formula for seeing through your mind and preparing it to receive a lesson in success.

"One day, I will be successful" is a simple idea that will jump-start your brain, helping it show you psychic imagery. This is like daydreaming, and it is easy and relaxing.

Just imagine, for imagination is the vehicle of your dreams. Your imagination will become progressively more visual. Eventually, it will be like watching a little television program playing inside your head. I have tried it, and it works. So practice picturing scenes, people, successes, relationships, business strategies that succeed, or places you want to be–all in your mind.

Think of something you wish for. For instance, imagine sitting in your favorite car "one day" and see what you would normally see as if you were really sitting in it. Look at the road on which you are driving; close your eyes and recreate it. Make it as realistic as you can. Immerse yourself in the imagery. If you can make it that real in your mind, the main thing becomes how you can achieve it. One day you will really have the same or a similar car.

Or try to jump-start your new business in your mind. Be a daydreamer, relax, have a drink, and convert your dream into reality. By taking control of your imagination, visualization, and mental imagery, you prepare your mind for a visual affirmation list. When you practice, it becomes perfect.

Your mind and third eye require a "warm-up" for them to kick into action and work consistently. It is like a car that has not been driven for a long time; it needs some reviving to get the engine humming again. So, take some time to think up a solution and to jump-start your new revolution.

Remember that you have gone through your entire life without having truly awakened and without using your psychic senses. You can do this by practicing using those senses on a regular basis or in a meditation once a week. You can't do this by surfing through forums or reading books endlessly.

Visualizing with your imagination and sensing the energy fields is a very easy thing to do. But you have to go about it in the right way—the positive way. It will never work if you are negative. Only positivity works! I am guiding you to do it this way for your own good and to help you to realize that there is something out there that you can try. The universal spirit will support you. It takes you only eight minutes a day to do it.

Forty-Three

Think Outside the Box

You have now gotten your hopes up, as you have taken that baby step. While reading this book, you have found the primary weakness that causes you to fail. Use my Baby Steps Method to delete an episode of failure from your life for good and to keep it from sabotaging your life. Do not leave things half done!

If you are still not sure about what I have said, stop whatever you are doing and think about the contents of this book. Think for a moment, and then start writing your affirmation list. Take action today. If you don't do it today, you never will.

Give yourself space. Do not expect to be Shakespeare from the first sentence. (Even Shakespeare rewrote.) Be yourself. Write a few sentences. Write a few more, and then more. Do not think what you have written is bad. It is not. It is only at the preliminary stage. You will go back to rewrite it, and after you have written a little more, you will continue to write more. It will get better after a few rounds of rewriting.

Knowledge is power, and if you apply it and interpret meaning correctly, you will make the right decisions. Think about what I have just said. Take your step this way, the positive way.

Be critical of your thinking. Think about what is important for you. Three of the most important things in life are relationships, success, and business. Of course, it may be hard to choose your thoughts at the beginning, but if you do not try now, you never will.

Did you know that the company with the most famous website in the world today encourages its staff to "just think" at least 30 percent of the time. That is what they are paid to do. Think creatively. You may need a quiet place to think, while others can think during rush hour. Just think. Alternatively, talk to someone close to you, and ask what is lacking in you. Do not be shy. Ask your friends lots of questions, and think about the answers.

Creative thinking works wonders for the successful mind and when making personal and business decisions. Just think, and think outside the box.

Forty-Four

Think Differently
You Can Become Rich and Successful

I once read a book at a friend's office (unfortunately, I can't remember its name) for which the two authors had investigated their neighbors to find out how people get wealthy. They surveyed millionaires who were simple, everyday people. These people who lived next door drove second-hand cars, shopped at the local grocery store, and lived in houses valued at less than US$1 million—and, of course, were all been paid for. The book was very successful because it appealed to a mass readership, showing us that we can all be millionaires. We just need to work on a simple strategy.

In fact, many people think that they can't be rich, and they focus on their destiny that way. They always stay in that mind-set. *You must not think that way.* Think differently, and you can become rich and successful simply because it is so easy. If your friend is rich, you too can try to become rich. However, success comes "one day."

Failure is a stepping stone to success.

Do what you love.

And believe in yourself.

It is possible to achieve your dreams!

Forty-Five

Can Chronically Ill People Become Successful?

Definitely yes!

I believe there are five things you must know to become a successful person:

1. finish the affirmation list,
2. know the definition of your purpose,
3. know what you really desire,
4. know what your goal is, and
5. have a burning anxiety to accomplish your goals.

First, you need to know the few simple attributes that can lead you to a successful and happy life. Honesty is necessary for true happiness. Dishonesty can never make a person happy. Self-discipline guarantees progress, wealth, prosperity, and success. It is the key to all progress.

A sick man can never hope to be happy, as his disease takes that away from him. The ability to feel young and the enjoyment of life are replaced by aches and pains, a bland taste in the mouth, and misery. Such people fear life. Instead, think positively; remove negativity from your head and your life. Read my book. Make sure you have a good diet, take your medicine as instructed, drink two liters of water daily, and exercise regularly. Meditation and living a tension-free life can also help you stay healthy and happy.

Above all, act now to get to know more people.

A wise person once said, "Thoughts alone are not enough to change the realities of our world. Action paves the way for the development of our lives." Do not hesitate to accept the challenges that come your way, and do not feel ashamed to dream an impossible dream. You were the one who dared to build castles in the air and to create those castles in reality. You can achieve. Dream big!

One day you will succeed.

Whether you are healthy or sick, I am sure you will succeed. As long you have a doctor who tells you that there is medicine for the illness, thank God and stay happy and successful. Never ever tell yourself that you are sick. Never. Always tell yourself, "I am fine." For me, this is like a medicine that keeps my body going and helps me healthy in my heart.

Take your every step in a positive way, and see yourself grow out of your fears, negative thoughts, and negative vibrations. And be filled with a positive mind, positive thoughts, and positive vibrations.

You will be a positive person and live life cheerfully. One day you will succeed in whatever you do.

Forty-Six

I Have Been Diagnosed with Lupus

What Should I Do Next?

I wrote the following article for the February 2013 of the Lupus Association (Singapore) Publication.

In life, we have two options: we can be miserable and ask, "Why must it happen to me?" or we can stay positive and be thankful for the things we still have.

I make an effort to stay optimistic and remain confident in the team of doctors and nurses that tend to me. Let me share my experience in discovering and managing my conditions, Systemic Lupus Erythematosus (SLE, or Lupus) and Antiphospholipid Syndrome (APS).

I can vividly recall the events that occurred five years ago, in June 2008. I was told that in order to save my life, my right leg had to be amputated. At that point, things were beyond my control. I did not suffer from hypertension, high cholesterol, diabetes, or heart or kidney problems; conditions that would have predisposed blockage of the vessels in my legs. However, my legs had become swollen, and over a period of three months, my right leg had become cold and numb due to poor blood circulation. I was advised by my doctors to have it amputated. It was a difficult decision as time was of essence, and I did not have much of a choice as my leg was deteriorating and beginning to darken due to the lack of proper blood circulation. When I was formally diagnosed with Lupus and APS, I slipped into depression and cried a lot during that trying period.

Slowly but surely, I decided to regain control of my life through small, positive steps. I made lists of the positive things in my life every day while I was admitted in the hospital, and steered my mind away from negative thoughts. I visualized the things that I could accomplish and convinced myself that I could achieve them. I imagined walking with the aid of my prosthetic leg and a black walking stick. This empowered me, and I managed to walk again seven months after my operation.

I began writing a book to motivate others through my experience. It has taken me six years to complete it, and I am now looking for a publisher in hope of providing a source of aid, encouragement and comfort to patients suffering the same fate as I have.

I started the Marina Bay Walking Meetup group on 4 June 2012. This walking group has approximately 2,700+ members from all walks of life at the time of writing. We walk every Saturday morning at various locations in Singapore. A month later, I founded the Walk for Lupus walking group. This group walks once a month at sunset hours. The walks are great opportunities for staying healthy and making friends. I am also a volunteer at the Lupus Association Singapore.

On World Lupus Day 2013, the Marina Bay Walking Meetup group walked 3.5 kilometers along the Marina Bay Waterfront Promenade. I feel that there is a need to create and increase public awareness about Lupus as few have heard of or have knowledge about it, unlike about common diseases such as cancer. It is also important for patients to explore ways to cope with the stress of suffering from Lupus. I believe that frequent exercise and relaxation would make it easier for lupus patients to battle the disease. Exercise not only reduces stress and lifts the mood, but also improves sleep. Stay active and positive always. May you be blessed with good health!

** Public awareness **

Forty-Seven

Thank You for Purchasing My First Book

I hope that one fine day, you too will say, "One day, I will be successful," that your dream will come true. Consider sharing this book with your friends, family, and children, and talk about how you can actively achieve success in the short term. You will understand, too, how to manage life successfully by being the person you have always wished to be.

I hope you have enjoyed the book so far and have learned something new from the One Day Method.

Let me ask you some questions:

- Have you ever wondered what is stopping you from achieving your dream?

- Have you ever wondered why you are missing out on a fulfilling career or relationship?

- Why have you so often felt stuck and uninspired?

- Open your mind and your eyes, and realize the truth: you have a unique mind. Do you believe it?

- Valuable knowledge is waiting to break out of its cocoon. Are you ready to receive it?

Imagine what your life would be like or how it would change if you could create a new destiny for yourself.

Nobody is born successful. Getting from where you are to where you want to be takes a lot of sacrifice, a lot of effort, and a lot of resilience, along with a lot of determination and planning.

You need to take that first baby step. Nobody else is going to do it for you, and I mean nobody. It is up to you only. It is not too late to start your dream and create a new destiny for yourself. Every person needs a push in the right direction—and that is the way, the positive way. Look for a process that will help you not only use the powerful mind that you have, but also gain a deep understanding of what miracles you can achieve for yourself and others.

Think about it for a moment.

Forty-Eight

Draft a Plan

You may be thinking, *How can I create a masterpiece or invent something?*

From the beginning of this book, I have asked you to dig deep. I am just asking you to try my One Day Method. Some people will not believe it, and some people will. If you don't believe it, how can you expect to make your dreams come true? Do you have the solution?

You are not reading this to be self-defeating. You are here because you want to be somebody. Success is closer to you than you think.

- Feel free to start dreaming of all the success that you would like to see for yourself in the future. You will be above the others, so practice leadership.

- Start writing your affirmation list. Scribble down all your wild thoughts.

- None of that can guarantees that you would be a success. The secret of the One Day Method is that visualization can help you achieve it.

- Understand your strengths and weaknesses, and use this wisdom to find and pursue a purpose for yourself.

- Share what you have learned thus far with your friends and family, and gain a deeper understanding of how to become a success.

For a typical "success" course, people are charged thousands of dollars in fees. However, all you have to do is learn the One Day Method, which can transform your current mind-set and help you develop a new future with a good lifestyle. And all it cost you is the price of this book. Is that not amazing?

Forty-Nine

Past, Present, and Future

If you want to know your past, what do you do? If you asked me, I might say, "Please look into your present moments. What do you see?"

You must let go of the old to make way for the new. But have you let it go? As the saying goes, "The old way is gone and will never come back again." If you understood this right now and take baby steps and use the One Day Method to achieve your wishes, I am sure you will position yourself for lasting success.

This world doesn't owe you anything. So stop daydreaming and start your action plan. First, draft your plan, write down your affirmation to-do list, and do your mediation once or twice a week. Create life for yourself, and stay happy always. Take full responsibility for your life. As you are the most important person and you are needed in this world, do it right now. It's too late to sit around and wait for somebody to do something someday. Someday is now!

Wake up from your daydreaming. Start *living* your life *today*! Somebody in the world needs *you*. Don't be afraid of it. Be afraid of a life you never lived because you were scared to take the first step of freedom.

Live your life *today*—not tomorrow, but today!

Don't ignore death, but don't be afraid of it either. The greatest loss is what dies inside you while you're still alive.

Be strong. Stand up and face the world with respect and dignity. Be bold. Be courageous. Be scared to death, and then take the next step anyway. Your life is yours only—but respect your family members too. Others can try to tell you, but they can't decide for you. The mind you have is yours only—not others'. They can walk with you, but not in your shoes. So make sure the path you decide to walk aligns with your heart and mind, and don't be scared to switch paths if you are not comfortable at this moment.

Remember, be humble and calm. When you are humble, your focus is much clearer.

Realize that this is your life. If life teaches you only one thing, let it be that taking a passionate leap is always worth it. Even if you have no idea where you're going to land, be brave enough to step up to the edge and listen to your heart. Motivate yourself and imagine a successful life. You can manifest something good just for yourself; you just need to visualize it sincerely and honestly.

Fifty

An Invitation

When you are in Singapore on a holiday, do join Marina Bay Walking Group under Meetup.com for our walks. (Be sure to RSVP.) Every Saturday morning we walk at different locations in Singapore. We would like to get to know our new friends better.

And remember to try my One Day Method and positive words. The law of natural attraction will come into your life, your soul, and your mind from the Superior God All-Mighty. I always feel God is the light that shows us the way, and God will show you the right way, for there is nothing that God can't do.

Prayer releases the power and wisdom of God into a situation. Calmness is the way we show our trust in God.

Miracles happen every day and every hour. We do our best, and God does the rest.

Believe in yourself.

Appendix 1

A Special Message

Walk for Miles, Walk for Smiles

We all join the walking group for a variety of reasons. The most obvious among them is, of course, for the exercise. For many, walking is not as "breathtaking" as running, but it still gets their hearts pumping and sweat glands working, and it gives us a reason to get into those Adidas gears we have relegated to cupboard exhibits for far too long.

Along the way, however, I'm sure we've all come to discover and gained more than we have imagined.

Throughout my year with the group, I have seen many people come and go, quite a few of whom never to return. However, there were even more who stuck around and became die-hard walkers till this day. Many have forged friendships among themselves that take them beyond the weekly walks. There's a pair of BFFs (Best Friends Forever) whose search for food places all over Singapore can give Makan Sutra and Dr. Leslie Tan a run for their money. We have bowling buddies competing in knocking pins down and cleaning the drains. We even have a couple of ladies who extended this spirit of camaraderie to others with their own meet up group, reaching even more people who are seeking to have fun together in a community. Inexperienced as they were when they started, there is every indication on their meet up page, Facebook photos and from my 'cameos' at a few of their events that their group is a great success as well.

From a recent conversation with Marina Bay Walkers' main organizer, Haresh, I recalled looking like I was owed a million dollars when I first joined the walk. I had been through some rough patches in life prior to joining the group and was trying to work through things. When I saw this "Marina Bay 3.5km Walking Group' on Meetup. com one day, I was bemused. "Somebody actually sets up a meet up group just to take a stroll together?" I thought. But since it was free and had no strings attached, I gave it a try. One year later, I'm still walking with the group. Throughout the year, the walks became more varied, covering various parts of Singapore, and the nature of the walks changed as well. We'd walk jungles when we've had enough of concrete and glass; we did vertical walks when we needed a break from the horizontal ones. We've tried food at many different places where we previously wouldn't have known or gone to on our own. Case in point: How many of us have been to the 'Best Prata Shop in Singapore' before?

When all's said and done, however, the one thing that took this group beyond its first birthday and kept it going and growing is the people. None of the above would have happened if not for the members of the Marina Bay Walkers. People from all walks of life simply came together to share and exchange graciously and unselfishly, which kept the walks fun and interesting. It is also the one thing that continues to draw new participants into the group.

Case in point #2: The Dempsey Hill walk saw more than 60 people turn up, outgunning the attendance for the previous record-setter, the Treetop Walk@MacRitchie, which had a few members short of 60.

I have also come to know of some who, like I had been, were working through some unpleasant moments life has dealt them. With each passing walk, however, the smiles on their faces grew more evident and brighter, and some even went from being passive to tossing ideas around for the group's activities. Whatever the reasons we have for being here, the smiles that we take away at the end of the day have given the group and its activities a lot more meaning beyond the physical benefits.

Because it is something we can never buy.

(Posted by Edward Seah, co-organizer of the Marina Bay Walking Meetup group since August 30, 2012.)

Please visit the site. Marina Bay Walking Group under Meetup.com and **http://www.wordtraders.net/2013/07/walk-for-miles-walk-for-smiles.html**

Appendix 2

A Walking Member

I stumbled upon the Marina-Bay-Walking-Meetup-Stay-healthy-Live-longer while browsing through the walking groups on www.meetup.com. This group is blessed to have many talented and dedicated co-organizers to keep the group active!

What attracted me to join the group were the cool one-of-a-kind walks: heritage walk in Bukit Brown, hidden reservoirs and marathon walk between MRT stations. The many beautiful pictures posted by members in the photos section played their role in enticing me to join the group. Treasure hunts and online quizzes give participants a mental workout and also add a surprise element to the group.

This is a hit as don't you just love surprises!?!

My special moments with Marina Bay walking meetup group are numerous and many more are being created when I attend more walking meetup. With unique individuals walking together, stories are shared and special moments created. Sure, there can be awkward moments when personalities clash and wavelengths differ.

But fret not, it is a walk after all.

You can always walk a little faster (brisk walk) or stop to smell the roses or take a picture of the beautiful scenery.

Just to diffuse the tension.

The best route that still lingers in my mind, up to this moment, is the one from Hilton hotel to Dempsey Hill via Minden Road in Singapore. The walk to Dempsey is lovely with much greenery everywhere! Good for your eyesight! The buildings along the route boast ancient architecture and provide a great backdrop for taking photos. The people in this walk were friendly and even offered to take a picture for me with the wooden Merlion. It is a happy coincidence I met some friends I made from earlier walks and from elsewhere during this particular walk.

Walk on! Walking in a group enriches you holistically.

Wonderful
Awesome
Lucid
Kind
Extraordinary
Realistic

(By Jane Ang [Junior], who has been a walking member of the Marina Bay Walking Meetup group since November 4, 2012.

The Final Word

Thanks to the creators of the Internet, I can now share my knowledge of and experiences with my One Day Method through this book, which can be kept handy in your heart and in your mind.

I hope that you have understood what I have said and that the final chapter is even more enticing than the opening lines, convincing you that you have made the right choice in choosing this book.

Thank you for reading my first book. You are welcome to write to me directly by e-mail: hareshbuxani@onedaysuccessful.com

Should you have any inquiries about the contents of my book, please send me an email, and I will reply to you as soon as possible. If you feel I have written something inappropriate, kindly accept my apologies, as I am new at this. And if you like my book, I would appreciate hearing your comments.

Thank you once again, and may God bless you with good health as well as a good, long life filled with abundance, laughter, love, prosperity, and success.

Remember, you need to visualize success in order to succeed in life.

Yes, it is possible!

It *works!*
Now it's your turn to try it.

Remember,
you need to visualize success in order to succeed in life.

Yes, it is possible.

About the Author

Haresh J. Buxani was born in Malaysia forty-nine years ago. He is an entrepreneur with a low-profile personality, as well as being an investor, adviser, and author. He is best known for understanding the "whats" and "hows" of real estate investing. His life is focused on and dedicated to investing strategically as a commercial investor, and he is best known for the good advice he gives to his friends and others. He is widely regarded as a successful and down-to-earth person.

Haresh started his career as an office boy and later became a salesman. After many years, he is still a commercial property investor for his family's real estate business in Asia. He achieved success by understanding what real life really is and from meditation, theory, and philosophical knowledge.

He understands the meaning of life from his marital problems and serious medical issues. Therefore, he decided to write this book, his first, which may become his first major success. He expects to launch his first multimillion-dollar enterprise should the book appeal to people. He will be writing a variety of books in the coming years and will probably be launching many more books and ebooks.

Haresh runs a voluntary walking group every Saturday morning for healthy people and for people living with illnesses, as walking is good for health. He is the organizer for the Marina Bay Walking Group on Meetup. com, and since July 2012, he also organized the Walk for Lupus at sunset hours on Marina Bay Waterfront Promenade and along Labrador Park in Singapore. He is also a volunteer for the Lupus Association (Singapore).

Haresh took almost six years to complete *One Day, I Will Be Successful*. All this happened three months and eleven days after he was diagnosed with a severe illness. He started writing the first page in 2008 and completed the book in 2014. In it he shares from his experiences about how to become a successful person, even if you've been through difficult situations.

Haresh has a loving family that supports him amid the mysteries of his life as well as the many hardships he has had to endure, such as the illness that made him what he is today.

He has passed the University of Life with flying colors.

* * *

Thank you to Sydney Felicio, my online book publisher under Partridge Publishing House.

Thank you to all members in the Editorial Department at Partridge Publishing. A Penguin Random House Company. Thank you very much.